English Grammar for Students of Arabic

The Study Guide for Those Learning Arabic

Ernest N. McCarus
University of Michigan

Second Edition

The Olivia and Hill Press®

The O&H Study Guides
Jacqueline Morton, editor

English Grammar for Students of Spanish
English Grammar for Students of French
English Grammar for Students of German
English Grammar for Students of Italian
English Grammar for Students of Latin
English Grammar for Students of Russian
English Grammar for Students of Japanese
English Grammar for Students of Arabic
English Grammar for Students of Chinese
Gramática española para estudiantes de inglés

Printed in the U.S.A.

ISBN: 978-0-934034-59-3

Library of Congress Control Number: 2021931335

CONTENTS

Introduction 1
Transcription of Arabic alphabet 3
1. What's in a Word? 5
   Meaning 5
   Parts of speech 5
   Form: word parts 6
   Function 9
   Agreement 9
2. What is a Noun? 11
3. What is Meant by Gender? 13
4. What is Meant by Number 16
5. What is Meant by Case? 20
   Function of words 20
   Declension 24
6. What is an Article? 25
   Definite articles 25
   Indefinite articles 26
   Concrete vs. abstract nouns 27
7. What is the Possessive? 29
8. What is a Subject? 32
9. What is a Predicate Word? 34
10. What are Objects? 36
   Direct and indirect objects 36
   Sentences with a direct and an indirect object 37
   Object of a preposition 39
11. What is an Adjective? 40
12. What is a Descriptive Adjective? 42
13. What is Meant by Comparison of Adjectives? 45
14. What is a Possessive Adjective? 50
15. What is an Interrogative Adjective? 52
16. What is a Demonstrative Adjective? 54
17. What is a Pronoun? 55
18. What is a Subject Pronoun? 57
19. What is an Object Pronoun? 62
20. What is an Interrogative Pronoun? 65
   Dangling prepositions 66
21. What is a Possessive Pronoun? 68
22. What is a Reflexive Pronoun? 70
23. What is a Demonstrative Pronoun? 72
24. What is a Relative Pronoun? 77
   Combining sentences with relative pronouns 78

25. What is a Verb? 84
26. What are the Principal Parts of a Verb? 88
27. What is a Verb Conjugation? 90
28. What are Infinitives and Gerunds? 93
29. What is a Participle? 95
30. What is an Auxiliary Verb? 99
Modals 101
31. What is Meant by Tense? 103
32. What is the Present Tense? 106
33. What is the Past Tense? 109
34. What is the Future Tense 113
Future of probability 114
Future-in-the-past 115
35. What are the Perfect Tenses? 117
The present perfect 117
The past perfect 118
The future perfect 119
36. What are the Progressive Tenses? 121
37. What is Meant by Active and Passive Voice? 123
38. What is Meant by Mood? 126
39. What is the Subjunctive Mood? 128
40. What is the Imperative Mood? 131
41. What is a Preposition? 135
42. What is an Adverb? 138
43. What is a Conjunction? 140
44. What are Phrases, Clauses and Sentences? 145
What is a phrase? 145
What is a clause? 146
What is a sentence? 147
45 What are Conditional Sentences? 149
46. What are Affirmative, Negative, Declarative and Interrogative Sentences? 153
Affirmative and negative 153
Declarative and interrogative 155
Tags 156
47. What is Meant by Direct and Indirect Statements? 158
48. What is Meant by Direct and indirect Questions? 160
Index 163

INTRODUCTION

English Grammar for Students of Arabic introduces you to the English grammar that will be useful for learning Arabic. Each grammatical term and structure is defined and its usage illustrated in both English and Arabic, pointing out similarities and differences and alerting you to common pitfalls. Once you understand the terms and concepts as they apply to your own language, it will be easier for you to understand what is being introduced in your textbook and by your teacher.

The Arabic dealt with here is Modern Standard Arabic, the written and spoken language of formal communication. It does not parallel any particular textbook and may serve as a complement to any Arabic course. As textbooks for the colloquial Arabic dialects (Egyptian, Moroccan, Levantine, Iraqi, etc.) use essentially the same grammatical terminology, this handbook is equally suitable for colloquial Arabic programs.

STUDY GUIDE

BEFORE DOING AN ASSIGNMENT — Read the sections in *English Grammar* and in your textbook that cover the topics you are going to study.

HOMEWORK — Take notes as you study your textbook. Highlighting is not sufficient. The more often you write down and use vocabulary and rules, the easier it will be for you to remember them. Oral activities should be done over several short periods of time rather than in one long session.

WRITTEN EXERCISES — As you write Arabic words or sentences say them out loud. Each time you write, read, say and hear a word it reinforces it in your memory.

IN CLASS — Take notes. You will know what the teacher considers important and it will help you remember what is being taught.

OBJECTIVE — You have learned something successfully when you are able to take a blank sheet of paper and write a short sentence in Arabic using the correct form of the Arabic words without reference to a textbook or dictionary. The tips below will help you with this learning process.

TIPS FOR LEARNING VOCABULARY

There are very few words that are common to English and Arabic. However, the root and pattern system of Arabic described in *What's in a Word?* on pp. 7-8 will greatly facilitate your learning of vocabulary (and you might even find it fun).

FLASHCARDS — Flashcards are a good, handy tool for learning new words and their meaning. You can carry them with you, group them as you wish and add information as you advance. Creating your own flashcards is an important first step in learning vocabulary.

1. Write the Arabic word or expression on one side of an index card and its English equivalent on the other side.
2. On the Arabic side include any information relevant to the word in question. For example, the root of the word (see p. 7) and its pattern (see p. 8).
3. On the Arabic side add a short sentence using the word or expression; it will be easier for you to recall a word in context. To make sure that your sentence is grammatically correct, copy an example from your textbook. For review purposes, note down the chapter and page number of your textbook where the word is introduced.

HOW TO USE THE CARDS — Regardless of the side you're working on, always say the Arabic word aloud.

1. Look at the Arabic side first. Going from Arabic to English is easier than from English to Arabic because it only requires your recognizing the Arabic word. Read the Arabic word(s) out loud, giving the English equivalent, then check your answer on the English side.
2. When you go easily from Arabic to English, turn the cards to the English side. Going from English to Arabic is harder than going from Arabic to English because you have to pull the word and its spelling out of your memory. Say the Arabic equivalent out loud as you write it down, then check the spelling. Some students prefer closing their eyes and visualizing the Arabic word and its spelling.
3. As you progress, put aside the cards you know and concentrate on the ones you still don't know.

TRANSCRIPTION OF ARABIC ALPHABET

In this handbook Arabic words are given in their most complete form, called the **CONTEXTUAL FORM**, as opposed to the **PAUSAL FORM** of Arabic where the final short vowels of words are dropped when the speaker pauses. In addition, hyphens will help you identify the various elements that make up Arabic words.

Arabic script	Transcription
ا	' ; ā
ب	b
ت	t
ث	th
ج	j
ح	ḥ
خ	kh
د	d
ذ	dh
ر	r
ز	z
س	s
ش	sh
ص	ṣ
ض	ḍ
ط	ṭ
ظ	ḍh
ع	ᶜ
غ	gh
ف	f
ق	q
ك	k
ل	l
م	m
ن	n
ه	h
و	w ; ū
ي	y ; ī
ء	' (**hamza**) (همزة)
ة	-atun, -a (**tā' marbūta** (تاء مربوطة)

Short vowels: ´ a (**fatḥa**); ʼ u (**ḍamma**); ˏ i (**kasra**)
(فتحه) (ضمة) (كسرة)

CHAPTER 1

WHAT'S IN A WORD?

When you learn a foreign language, in this case Arabic, you must look at each word in five ways: **MEANING, PART OF SPEECH, FORM, FUNCTION,** and **AGREEMENT**.

MEANING

An English word may correspond to an Arabic word that has a similar meaning:

Book has the same meaning as the Arabic word **kitāb**(كتاب).

Words with equivalent meanings are learned by memorizing **VOCABULARY**. While English and other European languages have borrowed words extensively from one another, English and Arabic share very few words; exceptions would be *alcohol* derived from **al-kuḥūl** (الكُحول) and *algebra* from **al-jabr** (الجَبر), and the Arabic word **bāṣ** (باص) derived from *bus.* Consequently, you will not be able to rely on similarities to English to guess the meaning of Arabic words.

CAREFUL — Arabic, like every other language, has expressions in which the meaning of a group of words is different from the meaning of the words taken individually. These are called **IDIOMATIC EXPRESSIONS** or **IDIOMS**. For instance, *"to fall* asleep" and *"to take* a walk" are English expressions where "to fall" and "to take" do not have their usual meaning as in *"to fall* down the stairs" or *"to take* a book to class." You will have to be on the alert for these idioms because they cannot be translated word-for-word in Arabic. For example, *he took* is **'a<u>kh</u>a<u>dh</u>a** (أخذ), but *he took a walk* is **tama<u>shsh</u>ā** (تمَشّى); *he fell* is **waqa'a** (وَقَعَ), but *he fell asleep* is **nāma** (نامَ).

PARTS OF SPEECH

In English and Arabic words are grouped according to the **PART OF SPEECH** to which they belong. Each part of speech has its own rules for spelling, pronunciation, word formation and use. This handbook covers the eight English parts of speech:

nouns	adverbs
verbs	prepositions
pronouns	conjunctions
adjectives	articles

Some parts of speech are further broken down according to type. Pronouns, for instance, can be personal, relative, interrogative, demonstrative or possessive.

In English and Arabic, there is another part of speech called **INTERJECTIONS** that is not covered in this handbook. These are exclamations such as "Oh!," "Dear me!" and "Alas!" Interjections do not require any grammatical knowledge, just memorization as vocabulary.

Arabic has a separate part of speech called **PARTICLES**; these words are characterized by the fact that they never change form. This handbook and your textbook will introduce you to the many Arabic particles.

In order to choose the correct Arabic equivalent of an English word, you will have to identify its part of speech. For example, look at the word *talk* in the following sentences. In each sentence it belongs to a different part of speech, each of which corresponds to a different Arabic word.

I went to a *talk* on Islam.
noun → **muḥāḍaratun** (مُحاضرةٌ)

They *talk* Arabic together.
verb → **yatakallamāni** (يتكلَّمانِ)

The various sections of this handbook show you how to identify parts of speech so that you are able to choose the proper Arabic words and the rules that apply to them.

FORM: WORD PARTS

In English and in Arabic words can be composed of various parts.

STEM — The stem is the part of the word which gives the word its meaning; for example, *day, view, cover, good, usual.*

PREFIX — A prefix refers to a group of letters which can be added before a stem to change its meaning or to give it an additional one. For example, the prefix *un-* changes the meaning of the stem to its opposite: *un- + usual → unusual, un- + cover → uncover;* the prefix *pre-* adds the meaning "before" to the stem: *pre- + paid → prepaid, pre- + view → preview.*

SUFFIX — A suffix refers to a group of letters that can be added to the end of a stem to give it an additional meaning or to change its part of speech. For example, the suffix *-ly* adds the meaning "every" to certain stems: *day + -ly → daily, year + -ly → yearly*; the suffix *-ness* changes the part of speech of the word *good* (an adjective, see p. 40) to *goodness* (a noun, see p. 11).

In English the stem is the dictionary form of the word and the use of prefixes and suffixes is limited. The most commonly used English prefixes are given under "prefix" above and the most commonly used suffixes are *-s, -er, -est* and *-ed* as in *book-s, small-er, small-est, walk-ed.*

In Arabic the majority of words make use of prefixes and suffixes.

ROOT — The root gives an Arabic word its basic meaning. It is usually made up of three consonants, called **RADICALS**, that appear in a fixed sequence in the stem. From a given root Arabic creates words with similarities in meaning belonging to different parts of speech. For instance, all the words containing **K** as the first radical, **T** as the second radical, and **B** as the third radical have something to do with *writing,* which is the basic meaning of the root **K-T-B**(كَتَبَ).

katab-a (كَتَبَ)	*he wrote* [verb: action of the root]
kitāb-u-n (كِتَابٌ)	*book* [noun: object related to writing]
ma**ktab**at-u-n (مَكْتَبَةٌ)	*library; bookstore* [noun: place where books are found]
kātib-u-n (كَاتِبٌ)	*writer, author* [noun: performer of the action of writing]

You will have to learn to identify the root of a word in order to look it up in the dictionary since words are not alphabetized according to their first letter, but according to the first consonant of their root. For example, all the words above are alphabetized under the letter "k" and the dictionary groups all the words derived from that root under the same entry.

STEM — The stem is the part of the Arabic word to which the the prefixes, suffixes and infixes (see "infix" below) are added. Thus the stem of **kitāb-un**(كِتَابٌ) *book* is **kitāb-**(كِتَاب); the hyphen indicates the end of the stem.

PREFIX, SUFFIX, INFIX — As in English, the meaning of Arabic words can be changed by adding prefixes and suffixes to the stem. In addition, Arabic words can also be changed with an **INFIX**, i.e., a consonant inserted inside the stem. For example, the consonant **-t-** inserted in a verb stem adds the meaning "oneself": **jamaʿū** (جَمعوا) *they collected (s. th.)* + **-t-** → **'i-j-tamaʿū** (اجتمعوا) *they collected themselves, i.e., they got together, they met.* (Since an Arabic sentence cannot start with a word beginning with two consonants, a glottal stop **hamza** (همزة) + a helping vowel is added as a prefix, in this instance **'i-** + **jtamaʿū** (اجتمعوا). The prefix is dropped when the word follows another word.)

As a result of the various kinds of prefixes, infixes and suffixes added to the stem, Arabic words are much more complex than English words.

a book	**kitāb-u-n** (كِتابٌ)	stem: **kitāb**-(كِتاب) + case ending (see p. 24): **-u** + nunation (see p. 26): **-n**
his book	**kitāb-u-hu**(كِتابُهُ)	stem: **kitāb**- (كِتاب)+ case ending: **-u** + possessive suffix (see p. 68): **-hu**

In this handbook there are hyphens separating the different parts of an Arabic word to help you identify its various components.

Pattern — The basic meaning of a root never changes; however, the meaning of a root can be expanded by inserting it within different patterns, each of which has its own meaning. A pattern is summarized by a formula indicating the sequence of consonants and vowels into which the radicals of the root are inserted. Such formulas use the letter "C" to indicate a consonant (two consecutive underlined "<u>CC</u>"indicate that the two consonants are the same), "v" indicates a short vowel and "vv" a long vowel; parentheses in a pattern indicate items that occur with some words but not with others.

Here is an example with different roots being inserted into a pattern called "noun of place"(**'ismu makān** (اسمُ مكانٍ) in Arabic). By inserting a root in that pattern you are indicating the place where the activity of that root takes place. The pattern is summarized as **maCCaC(a)**. In practice, this means adding **ma**-(مَ) before the first two root consonants (regardless of what they are), then adding the vowel **-a-** followed by the third consonant (whatever it is) of the root. The **(a)** stands for the suffix **-at-** which identifies feminine nouns (see *What is Meant by Gender?*, p. 13). The combination of root and pattern gives you the stem to which you will add the appropriate prefixes and suffixes (the hyphen at the end of the Arabic words below indicates that the word is incomplete).

Root	**Pattern maCCaC(a)**	
K-T-B(كتب) *write*	**maktab**-(مَكتب)	where writing is done: *office; desk*
S-K-N(سكن) *to reside*	**maskan**-(مَسكن)	where one resides: *residence, home*
D-R-S(درس) *study*	**madrasat**-(مَدرسة)	where one studies: *school*

If we insert the roots above into different patterns, we get other extended meanings. For example, by inserting the root **D-R-S** (درس) *study* in the pattern **Ca<u>CC</u>aC**, called "causative verb" (to cause someone to do the action of the root), we get **darras-a** (درّس) *to cause someone to study*, namely, *to instruct.*

Recognizing roots and patterns makes it easier to learn vocabulary.

FUNCTION

In English and Arabic the role a word plays in a sentence is called its **FUNCTION**. For example, words that are nouns can have the following functions:

subject
predicate
direct object
indirect object
object of preposition

In order to choose the correct form of the Arabic equivalent of an English word, you will not only have to identify its part of speech but also its function in the sentence. As an example, look at the word *teachers* in the following sentences. In each sentence *teachers* has a different function, each one requiring a different form in Arabic.

I know *the teachers.*

function → direct object (see p. 36) → **'al-muʿallim-īna** (المُعلّمين)

The teachers don't know me.

function → subject (see p. 32) → **'al-muʿallim-ūna** (المُعَلّمون)

The various sections of this handbook show you how to identify the functions of words so that you will be able to choose the proper Arabic words and the rules that apply to them.

AGREEMENT

In English and Arabic, a word can influence the form of another word, that is, it can change its spelling and pronunciation. This "matching" is called **AGREEMENT** and it is said that one word "agrees with" another.

I am	*am* agrees with *I*
you are	*are* agrees with *you*
she is	*is* agrees with *she*

Agreement does not play a big role in English, but it is an important part of the Arabic language. Look at the following examples where the English word *new* remains the same, but the Arabic equivalent changes in spelling and pronunciation: **'a-l-jadīdat-i** (الجديدةِ) when it refers to *student* (**'a-l-ṭālibat-i** (الطالبةِ)) and **'a-l-jadīd-u** (الجديدُ) when it refers to *book* (**'a-l-kitāb-u** (الكتابُ)).

the book of ***the new*** *student*

'a-l-jadīdat-i (الجديدةِ)

the new *book of the student*

'a-l-jadīd-u (الجديدُ)

As the various parts of speech are introduced in this handbook, we will go over agreement so that you will learn which words agree with other words and how the agreement is shown.

What's in a word: Arab, Arabic or Arabian?

In English there seems to be a good deal of confusion in the usage of the words "Arab," "Arabic" and "Arabian." While they are roughly synonymous, each word is specialized in its usage:

Arab — refers to people: *an Arab philosopher, Arab visitors, the Arab World, Arab culture.*

Arabic — refers to the Arabic language and its literature: *an Arabic poem, Arabic literature, Arabic dialects, Arabic music.*

Arabian — refers to the Arabian Peninsula and its inhabitants: *the Arabian Bedouin, Arabian tribes, an Arabian horse, the Arabian Saluki, the Arabian Desert, the Arabian Sea.*

Compare the following: *an Arab teacher*, an Arab who teaches an unspecified subject; *an Arabic teacher,* someone who teaches the Arabic language who might or might not be an Arab; *an Arabian teacher,* a teacher from the Arabian peninsula (Saudi, Kuwaiti, etc.).

CHAPTER 2

WHAT IS A NOUN?

A **NOUN** is a word that can be the name of a person, animal, place, thing, event or idea.

• a person	professor, prophet, student, girl Kahlil, Gibran, Ibrahim, Muhammad
• an animal	dog, bird, camel, snake Fido, Tweetie, Teddy, Rex
• a place	city, state, country, continent Beirut, Iraq, the Middle East, Luxor
• a thing	lamp, airplane, book, baklava the Sphinx, the Nile, Bible, Koran
• an event or activity	graduation, marriage, birth, growth football, robbery, rest, pilgrimage
• an idea or concept	poverty, democracy, humor, mathematics addition, strength, elegance, virtue

IN ENGLISH

As you can see in the examples above, a noun is not only a word that names something that is **CONCRETE**, such as a *table, dog* and *house,* it can also be the name of things that are **ABSTRACT**, such as *justice, jealousy* and *honor* (see *What is an Article?*, p. 25).

A noun that does not state the name of a specific person, place, thing, etc. is called a **COMMON NOUN.** A common noun does not begin with a capital letter unless it is the first word of a sentence. All the nouns above that are not capitalized are common nouns.

A noun that is the name of a specific person, place, thing, etc. is called a **PROPER NOUN**. A proper noun always begins with a capital letter. All the nouns above that are capitalized are proper nouns.

The teacher saw Majdi.

common noun (teacher) — proper noun (Majdi)

To help you learn to recognize nouns, look at the paragraph below where the nouns are in *italics.*

The *Near East* is the *home* of three major *religions: Judaism, Christianity* and *Islam,* and each has its own holy *book.* The *Torah,* which comes from a Hebrew *root* meaning *instruction* or *law,* is the *Bible* of the *Jews,* and the holy *book* of the *Christians* is called the "*Bible,*" which gets its *name* from the Phoenician *port* of *Byblos,* famous as the *seaport* from which *papyrus* was exported. The *Koran,* the holy *book* of *Islam,* gets its *name* from an Arabic *root* meaning "to recite" or "to read," since traditionally it is memorized and recited from *memory.*

IN ARABIC

As in English, Arabic nouns are the name of a person, animal, place, thing, event or idea. However, since Arabic script does not have capital and lower-case letters, there is no difference, for example, in the initial Arabic letters used for the common noun **laban** (لبن) *milk* and the proper noun **lubnān** (لبنان) *Lebanon.*

TERMS USED TO TALK ABOUT NOUNS

- **DICTIONARY FORM** — In Arabic, the form of a noun found in the dictionary is composed of the stem + the case ending **-u** + the indefinite article suffix **-n** (see the relevant chapters below).
- **STEM** — In English and Arabic, the stem is the part of the word that gives the word its meaning (see pp. 6-7 in *What's in a Word?).*
- **GENDER** — In Arabic, a noun has gender; that is, it can be classified according to whether it is masculine or feminine (see *What is Meant by Gender?,* p. 13).
- **NUMBER** — In English and Arabic, a noun has number; that is, it can be identified according to whether it is singular or plural (see *What is Meant by Number?,* p. 16).
- **FUNCTION** — In English and Arabic, a noun can have a variety of functions in a sentence; for example, it can be the subject of the sentence (see *What is a Subject?,* p. 32) or an object (see *What are Objects?,* p. 36).
- **CASE** — In Arabic, a noun's function in a sentence is indicated by a variety of endings (see *What is Meant by Case?,* p. 20).
- **DEFINITE OR INDEFINITE** — In English and Arabic, a noun can be classified as definite or indefinite; that is, whether it refers to a specified item or person or not (see *What is an Article?,* p. 25).

CHAPTER

3

WHAT IS MEANT BY GENDER?

GENDER in the grammatical sense means that a word can be classified as masculine, feminine, or neuter.

Did Salman give Amal the book?
Yes, *he* gave *it* to *her*.
masc. neuter fem.

Grammatical gender is not very important in English; however, it plays a major role in Arabic where the gender of a word is often reflected not only in the way the word itself is spelled and pronounced, but also in the way all the words agreeing with it are spelled and pronounced (see "agreement," p. 9).

More parts of speech have gender in Arabic than in English.

ENGLISH	**ARABIC**
pronouns	nouns
possessive adjectives	pronouns
	adjectives
	verbs

Since each part of speech follows its own rules to indicate gender, you will find gender discussed in the chapters dealing with pronouns, adjectives and verbs. In this chapter we shall only look at the gender of nouns.

IN ENGLISH

Nouns themselves do not have gender, but sometimes their meaning indicates a gender based on the biological sex of the person or animal the noun stands for. For example, when we replace a proper or common noun that refers to a man or a woman, we use *he* for males and *she* for females. There are a few feminine suffixes (see p. 6) that make the noun feminine, for example, *-ess* in *actress, princess, lioness* and *-ette* as in *brunette, drum majorette.*

- nouns referring to males indicate **MASCULINE** gender

Ali came home; *he* was tired, and I was glad to see *him.*
noun (male) masculine masculine

- nouns referring to females indicate **FEMININE** gender

  Amal came home; *she* was tired, and I was glad to see *her*.
  noun (female) — feminine — feminine

- nouns that do not have biological gender are considered **NEUTER** and are replaced by *it*

  The city of Cairo is lovely. I enjoyed visiting *it*.
  noun (place) — neuter

IN ARABIC

All nouns — common nouns and proper nouns — have gender; they are either masculine or feminine. The gender of an Arabic noun is based either on the biological sex of the noun, if it has one, or else on the suffix of the stem (see p. 6).

- nouns referring to humans or animals → gender based on the biological sex of the person or animal

MALES → MASCULINE	FEMALES → FEMININE
man	mother
prince	woman teacher
Caliph	princess
tiger	female cat

- all other nouns → gender based on the suffix at the end of the stem

  Stems that have a feminine suffix are feminine nouns. The most common feminine suffix is **-at-**.

kitāb**at**-u-n (كتابةٌ) (stem)	*writing; penmanship*
muhimm**at**-u-n (مهمّةٌ)	*mission, task*
dawl**at**-u-n (دولةٌ)	*country, nation*
ᶜawlam**at**-u-n (عَولمةٌ)	*globalization*
shamsiyy**at**-u-n (شمسيّةٌ)	*umbrella*

  Stems that don't have a feminine suffix are likely to be masculine nouns.

kitāb-u-n (كتابٌ) (stem)	*book*
maktab-u-n (مكتبٌ)	*office*
salām-u-n (سَلامٌ)	*peace*

Your textbook will introduce you to nouns whose gender does not fall into one of the above categories.

As you learn a new noun, you should always learn its gender because it will affect the spelling and pronunciation of the words related to it. Textbooks and dictionaries usually indicate the gender of a noun with an *m.* for masculine or an *f.* for feminine.

CHAPTER 4

WHAT IS MEANT BY NUMBER?

Number in the grammatical sense means that a word can be classified as singular or plural. When a word refers to one person or thing, it is said to be **singular**; when it refers to more than one, it is **plural**.

one *book*	two *books*
singular	plural

Number is not very important in English; however, it plays a major role in Arabic where the number of a word is often reflected not only in the way the word itself is spelled and pronounced, but also in the way all the words agreeing with it are spelled and pronounced (see "agreement," p. 9).

More parts of speech indicate number in English than in Arabic.

English	**Arabic**
nouns	nouns
pronouns	pronouns
verbs	verbs
demonstrative adjectives	adjectives
articles	

Since each part of speech follows its own rules to indicate number, you will find number discussed in the chapters dealing with articles, adjectives, pronouns and verbs. In this chapter we shall only look at number in nouns (see *What is a Noun?*, p. 11).

IN ENGLISH

A plural noun is usually spelled and pronounced differently from its singular form. A singular noun is made plural in one of two ways:

- a singular noun can add an *"-s"* or *"-es"*

book	book*s*
kiss	kiss*es*

- other singular nouns change their spelling

man	men
mouse	mice
leaf	leaves
child	children

IN ARABIC

Unlike English which has only two forms to indicate number, Arabic has three: 1. the singular form that refers to one item or person 2. the dual form that refers to two items or persons and 3. the plural form that refers to three or more items or persons. For all references to case endings and gender below see *What is Meant by Case?*, p. 20 and *What is Meant by Gender?*, p. 13.

SINGULAR — The singular form refers to one item or person. It consists of the singular stem + a case ending. The form listed in the dictionary is the singular form in the nominative case: singular stem + nominative case ending **-u** + the suffix **-n** indicating that the noun is indefinite (see p. 26).

a boy
walad-u-n, walad-i-n, walad-a-n (وَلَدٌ، وَلَدٍ ، وَلَداً)
- **walad** (وَلَد)-: masc. sing. stem
- **-u, -i, -a**: case endings → nom., gen., acc.
- **-n**: nunation → indefinite

a family
'usrat-u-n, 'usrat-i-n, 'usrat-a-n (أسرةٌ، أسرةٍ ، أسرةً)
- **'usrat** (أسرة)-: fem. sing. stem
- **-u, -i, -a**: case endings → nom., gen., acc.
- **-n**: nunation → indefinite

DUAL — The dual form refers to two items or persons. It is formed with the singular stem + dual suffix **-āni** (nom.) or **-ayni** (gen./acc.).

two boys
walad-āni, walad-ayni (ولدانِ ، ولدَينِ)
- **walad** (ولد) -: masc. sing. stem
- **-āni, -ayni:** case endings → nom., gen./acc.

two families
'usrat-āni, 'usrat-ayni (أسرتانِ ، أسرتينِ)
- **usrat** (أسرة)-: fem. sing. stem
- **-āni, -ayni:** case endings → nom., gen./acc.

PLURAL — The plural form refers to three or more items or persons. It is formed in one of two ways.

- **sound plurals** — The term "sound plurals" refers to nouns that make their plural by adding the sound plural suffixes to the singular stem.

MASC. PL. SUFFIXES ADDED TO STEM: **-ūna** (nom.), **-īna** (gen./acc.)
FEM. PL. SUFFIXES REPLACE -AT- ENDING OF SING.: **-āt-u-n** (nom.), **-āt-i-n** (gen./acc.).

teachers (men)
muʿallim-ūna, muʿallim-īna (مُعلّمونَ ، معلمين)
- **muʿallim** (مُعلّم)-: masc. sing. stem
- **-ūna, -īna**: gender, number, case endings → masc. pl. nom., gen./acc.

teachers (women)
muʿallimāt-u-n, muʿallimāt-i-n (مُعلّماتٌ ، معلماتٍ)
- **muʿallimāt**(مُعلّمات) -: fem. sing. stem → ʾ**muʿallima~~t~~** → **muʿallimāt**-(مُعلّمات) → fem. pl. stem
- **-u, -i**: case endings → nom., gen./acc.
- **-n**: nunation → indefinite

- **broken plurals** — The term "broken plurals" refers to nouns that make their plural form by changing the pattern of their singular stem and adding the singular case endings.

boys
ʾawlād-u-n, ʾawlād-i-n, ʾawlād-a-n (اوْلادٌ ، اولادٍ ، اولاداً)
Root: **W-L-D** *to give birth*
Sing. stem pattern: CaCaC → **walad** (ولد)- *boy*
Pl. stem pattern: ʾaCCāC → ʾ**awlād** (اولاد)- *boys*
- ʾ**awlād** (اولاد)-: pl. stem
- **-u, -i, -a**: sing. case endings → nom., gen., acc.
- **-n**: nunation → indefinite

books
kutub-u-n, kutub-i-n, kutub-a-n (كُتُبٌ ، كتبٍ ، كتباً)
Root: **K-T-B** *book*
Sing. stem pattern CiCāC: **kitāb** (كتاب) *book*
Pl. stem pattern CuCuC: **kutub** (كُتب)- *books*
- **kutub** (كُتب)-: pl. stem
- **-u, -i, -a**: sing. case endings → nom., gen., acc.
- **-n**: nunation → indefinite

Selecting the appropriate plural for a noun depends on three factors:

1. the gender of the noun
2. whether or not the noun refers to human beings
3. the pattern of the noun (see p. 8)

Your textbook will show you how to form broken plurals and identify the patterns that take sound or broken plurals (see p. 24 in *What is Meant by Case?*).

Collective nouns

In Arabic there is a category of nouns called **collective nouns** that is used to refer to certain materials and some plants and animals as groups in general.

Apples are healthy.
Cows provide milk and other dairy products.

The dictionary and your textbook will identify nouns that fall into the category of Arabic collective nouns.

While the English equivalent of Arabic collective nouns is in the plural, Arabic collective nouns are always masculine singular: **shajar-u-n** (شجرٌ) (masc. sing.) → *trees* (pl.).

When referring to one or more individual items of the group, collective nouns use a special form, called **NOUN OF UNITY**. To create a noun of unity, the feminine suffix **-at-** is added to the collective noun.

COLLECTIVE NOUN (masc. sing.)		**NOUN OF UNITY (fem. sing.)**	
mawz-u-n (موزٌ)	*bananas*	mawz**at**-u-n (موزةٌ)	*a banana*
shajar-u-n (شجرٌ)	*trees*	shajar**at**-u-n (شجرةٌ)	*a tree*
tuffāḥ-u-n (تفاحٌ)	*apples*	tuffāḥ**at**-u-n (تفاحةٌ)	*an apple*
baqar-u-n (بقرٌ)	*cows*	baqar**at**-u-n (بقرةٌ)	*a cow*

As nouns of unity refer to specific items, they can be made dual and plural like other feminine singular nouns.

Bananas *are good for you.*

collective → masc. sing. → **'al-mawz-u** (الموزُ)

The banana *I bought is ripe.*

nouns of unity → fem. sing. → **'al-mawzat-u** (الموزةُ)

He gave me ***two bananas****.*

noun of unity → dual → **mawzat-ayni** (موزتينِ)

He gave me ***eight bananas****.*

noun of unity → plural indefinite→ **mawzāt-i-n** (موزاتٍ)

CAREFUL — In order to choose the correct Arabic word, you will have to learn which Arabic nouns are collectives so that you will know that you should apply the rules specific to collectives.

CHAPTER

5

WHAT IS MEANT BY CASE?

CASE is the change in the form of a word to show how it functions within a sentence. This change of form usually takes place in the ending of the word; occasionally, the entire word changes.

I see Habib.
|
the person speaking;
function → subject

Habib sees *me*.
|
the person speaking;
function → object

In the sentences above, the person speaking is referred to by the forms "I" and "me." Different forms are used because in each sentence the person speaking has a different grammatical function. In the first sentence "I" is used because the person speaking is doing the "seeing" and in the second sentence "me" is used because the person speaking is the object of the "seeing."

More parts of speech are affected by case in Arabic than in English.

ENGLISH	**ARABIC**
nouns	nouns
pronouns	pronouns
	adjectives

Since each part of speech follows its own rules to indicate case, you will find case discussed in the chapters dealing with adjectives and pronouns. In this chapter we shall only look at case in nouns (see *What is a Noun?*, p. 11).

FUNCTIONS OF WORDS

The grammatical role of a word in a sentence is called its **FUNCTION**. The function is often based on the word's relationship to the verb (see *What is a Verb?*, p. 84). Here are some of the various functions that a noun can have, with reference to the chapter in this handbook where that function is studied in detail.

Subject — A noun or pronoun that performs the action of the verb (see *What is a Subject?*, p. 32 and *What is a Subject Pronoun?*, p. 57).
Predicate — A noun or adjective that is linked to the subject by a linking verb (see *What is a Predicate Word?*, p. 34).
Object — A noun or pronoun that is the receiver of the action of a verb (see *What are Objects?*, p. 36) or is governed by a preposition. There are different types of objects: direct objects (see p. 36) and indirect objects (see p. 36) of a verb and objects of a preposition (see p. 39).

Knowing how to analyze the function of words in an English sentence will help you to establish which case is required in the Arabic sentence.

IN ENGLISH

In English the form of a word rarely shows its function in a sentence. Usually it is word order, namely where a word is placed in the sentence, that indicates the meaning of the sentence.

> *Ahmad* saw *Zayd* in class.
> Ahmad did the seeing and Zayd is the one he saw.
>
> *Zayd* saw *Ahmad* in class.
> Zayd did the seeing and Ahmad is the one he saw.

By placing the nouns Ahmad and Zayd in different parts of the sentence we change the meaning of the sentence.

English personal pronouns are a good example of case in English, since their function is indicated not only by their place in a sentence, but also by their form, namely by their case (see *What is a Pronoun?*, p. 55).

> *I* know *them.*
> *They* know *me.*

We do not say, "I know *they*" or "They know *I*" because the forms *they* and *I* can only be used to refer to the doer of the action, the subject, whereas *them* and *me* can only be used to refer to the object of the action.

In English, there are three cases: the subjective, the objective and the possessive.

Subjective case — The case used for personal pronouns that function as subjects or predicates (see *What is a Subject Pronoun?*, p. 57 and *What is a Predicate Word?*, p. 34).

He saw Fatima.
personal pronoun
subject → subjective case

It is *he.*
personal pronoun
predicate word → subjective case

Objective case — The case used for personal pronouns that function as objects (see *What is an Object Pronoun?*, p. 62).

Fatima saw *him.*
personal pronoun
object → objective case

Possessive case — The case used for personal pronouns and for nouns to indicate possession (see *What is a Possessive Pronoun?*, p. 68 and *What is the Possessive?*, p. 29).

Fatima didn't find *her* book, so she took *his.*
personal pronouns
possessor → possessive pronoun

The teacher found *Fatima's* book.
possessor
possessive case of noun

IN ARABIC

As in English, words appear in a sentence according to certain rules. In addition, Arabic nouns, pronouns and adjectives take different endings, called **case endings** or **inflections**, that indicate their function in the sentence. You will find case discussed in the chapters dealing with adjectives and pronouns. In this chapter we shall only look at the case system of nouns.

Arabic nouns, pronouns and adjectives have three cases: nominative, accusative and genitive.

Nominative case — Like the English subjective, the nominative is used for the subject of the sentence and for the predicate in verbless sentences (see p. 34 in *What is a Predicate Word?* and p. 147 in *What are Phrases, Clauses and Sentences?*). It is the form of the word listed in the dictionary. The nominative case ending is **-u**.

***The exam** is long but easy.*
subject → nominative → **'a-l-imtiḥān-u** (الامتحانُ)
stem nominative

The visitor [is] ***a student*** *in this class.*
predicate → nominative → **ṭālib-u**-n (طالِبٌ)
stem nominative + nunation

GENITIVE CASE — Like the English possessive, the genitive is used to show possession. It is also used for objects of prepositions such as **min** (مِن) *from* and **maᶜa** (مَعَ) *with* (see *What is a Preposition?*, p. 135). The genitive case ending is **-i**.

*This is **the teacher's** book.*

possessive noun → genitive → **'a-l-muᶜallim-i** (المُعلّمِ)

*Let's all go talk **with the instructor**.*

object of preposition **maᶜa** (مَعَ) *with* →genitive →**'a-l-mudarris-i** (المُدرِّسِ)

The genitive is used to express the equivalent of the English preposition *of* as part of a structure called **THE GENITIVE CONSTRUCT.** This structure is composed of a noun in a case appropriate to its function in the sentence + a noun in the genitive case. The first noun, called the 1st term of the genitive construct, is automatically definite and cannot take the definite article. The second noun, called the 2nd term of the genitive construct, is in the genitive.

*Where is the capital of **Iraq**?*
'ayna ᶜāṣimat-u **-l-ᶜirāq-i**? (أينَ عاصمةُ العراقِ؟)

- **'ayna** (أينَ) *where?:* interrogative adverb
- **ᶜāṣimatu** (عاصِمةُ) *(the) capital:* noun, fem. sing., subj. in verbless sentence → nom., 1st term in gen. construct → def.
- **-l-ᶜirāqi** (العراقِ) *(of) Iraq:* proper noun, masc. sing. def. , 2nd term in gen. construct → gen.

For more on the genitive construct see p. 30 in *What is the Possessive?*.

ACCUSATIVE CASE — Like the English objective, the accusative is used for the object of a verb. It is also used for many expressions such as expressions of time, place, manner, degree, etc. The accusative case ending is **-a**.

*Have you seen **the professor**?*

object of verb *seen* → accusative → **'al-'ustā<u>dh</u>-a** (الاستاذَ)

*Yes, I saw him **today**.*

expression of time → accusative → **'al-yawm-a** (اليومَ)

*I've seen him **more** than once.*

expression of degree → accusative → **'ak<u>th</u>ar-a** (أكثرَ)

Your textbook will identify other uses of the accusative.

Declension

The complete set of case endings for nouns, pronouns and adjectives is called a **declension**. There are two basic declensions, one for nouns that take sound plurals and one for nouns that take broken plurals (see pp. 17-8 in *What is Meant by Number?*). The following characteristics are common to both declensions:

1. the three-case set of endings: **-u** (nom.), **-i** (gen.), **-a** (acc.)
2. the indefinite article suffix **-n** added to the endings above when the noun is indefinite (see p. 26 in *What is an Article?*)
3. the dual case endings: **-āni** (nom.), **-ayni** (gen./acc).

Here are examples of the sound plural and broken plural declensions.

- **sound plurals** — masculine nouns → same singular stem for singular and plural + different case endings for singular and plural; feminine nouns in **-at-** → change **-at-** to **-āt-** and take the two-case set of endings, **-u** (nom.), **-a** (gen./acc.)

Masc. sing. stem: mudarris- (مُدرس) *male instructor*
Fem. sing. stem: mudarrisat-(مُدرسات) *female instructor*

<table>
<tr><th></th><th></th><th>Singular</th><th>Dual</th><th>Plural</th></tr>
<tr><td rowspan="2">Nominative</td><td>(masc.)</td><td>mudarris-u-n (مُدرسٌ)</td><td>mudarris-āni (مُدرسانِ)</td><td>mudarris-ūna (مدرسونَ)</td></tr>
<tr><td>(fem.)</td><td>mudarrisat-u-n (مُدرسةٌ)</td><td>mudarrisat-āni (مُدرستانِ)</td><td>mudarrisāt-u-n (مدرساتٌ)</td></tr>
<tr><td rowspan="2">Genitive</td><td>(masc.)</td><td>mudarris-i-n (مُدرسٍ)</td><td rowspan="4">mudarris-ayni (مُدرسينِ)
mudarrisat-ayni (مُدرستينِ)</td><td rowspan="4">mudarris-īna (مدرسينَ)
mudarrisat-a-n (مدرساتً)</td></tr>
<tr><td>(fem.)</td><td>mudarrisat-i-n (مُدرسةٍ)</td></tr>
<tr><td rowspan="2">Accusative</td><td>(masc.)</td><td>mudarris-a-n (مُدرساً)</td></tr>
<tr><td>(fem.)</td><td>mudarrisāt-i-n (مُدرسةً)</td></tr>
</table>

- **broken plurals** — different stems for the singular and plural + singular case endings.

Sing. stem: kitāb- (كتاب) (masc.) *book*
Pl. stem: kutub- (كُتب) (fem. sing.) *books*

<table>
<tr><th></th><th>Singular</th><th>Dual</th><th>Plural</th></tr>
<tr><td>Nominative</td><td>kitāb-u-n (كِتابٌ)</td><td>kitāb-āni (كِتابانِ)</td><td>kutub-u-n (كُتُبٌ)</td></tr>
<tr><td>Genitive</td><td>kitāb-i-n (كِتابٍ)</td><td rowspan="2">kitāb-ayni (كِتابينِ)</td><td>kutub-i-n (كُتبٍ)</td></tr>
<tr><td>Accusative</td><td>kitāb-a-n (كِتابًا)</td><td>kutub-a-n (كُتباً)</td></tr>
</table>

Your textbook will present the various declensions of nouns, pronouns and adjectives.

CHAPTER 6

WHAT IS AN ARTICLE?

An **ARTICLE** is a word placed before a noun to show whether the noun refers to a specific person, animal, place, thing, event or idea, or whether it refers to a non-specific person, thing, or idea.

I saw *the* boy you spoke about.
a specific boy

I saw *a* boy in the street.
not a specific boy

In English and Arabic there are two types of articles: **DEFINITE ARTICLES** and **INDEFINITE ARTICLES.**

DEFINITE ARTICLES

IN ENGLISH

A **DEFINITE ARTICLE** is used before a noun when we are speaking about a person, animal, thing, or idea that has already been referred to. There is one definite article: *the.*

I read *the* book you recommended.
a specific book

I ate *the* apple you gave me.
a specific apple

IN ARABIC

As in English, a definite article is used before a noun, referred to as a **DEFINITE NOUN,** when we are speaking about a specified person, place, animal, thing, or idea. In Arabic, the definite article **-l-** is added at the beginning of the noun. The definite article never changes form. Since a word pronounced in isolation or at the beginning of a sentence cannot start with two consonants, the definite article **-l-** is preceded by a glottal stop (ʼ) + the helping vowel **a** (**ʼa-l-**) in those two instances. In most textbooks the definite article is presented as **al-**.

ʼa-l-kitāb-u (الكتابُ)	*The book*
wa-**l**-kitāb-u (والكتابُ)	*... and the book*

'a-l-tuffāḥat-u (التفاحةُ)	*The apple*
wa-**l-tuffāḥat-u** (والتفاحةُ)	*... and the apple*
'a-l-kutub-u (الكتبُ)	*The books*
wa -**l**-kutub-u (والكتبُ)	*... and the apples*

INDEFINITE ARTICLES

IN ENGLISH

An **INDEFINITE ARTICLE** is used before a noun when we are not speaking about a specified person, animal, place, thing, event, or idea. There are two indefinite articles: *a* and *an.*

- *a* is used before a word beginning with a consonant

  I saw *a* boy in the street.
  not a specific boy

- *an* is used before a word beginning with a vowel

  I ate *an* apple.
  not a specific apple

The indefinite article is used only with a singular noun. To indicate a nonspecified plural noun the word *some* can be used.

I saw boys in the street.
I saw *(some)* boys in the street.

I ate apples.
I ate *(some)* apples.

IN ARABIC

As in English, an **INDEFINITE NOUN**, i.e., a noun not previously referred to, may take an indefinite article. The indefinite article is the suffix **-n** that is added after the case ending when the case ending consists of a single vowel: **-u**, **-i** or **-a** (see *What Is Meant by Case?*, 20). This consonant is called **NUNATION**, based on the Arabic name of the letter "n," **nūn**.

kitāb-u-**n** (كتابٌ)	***a*** *book*
kutub-u-**n** (كتبٌ)	***some*** *books*

broken plural (see p. 18)

tuffāḥat-u-**n** (تفاحةٌ)	***an*** *apple*
tuffāḥāt-u-**n** (تفاحاتٌ)	***some*** *apples*

feminine sound plural (see p. 17)

As a general rule, Arabic nouns are indefinite unless there is a factor that makes them definite, such as the presence of the definite article or a following noun in the genitive case (see the genitive construct, pp. 23, 30). Refer to your textbook for instances when nunation is avoided.

Remember that Arabic nouns are identified by their gender (masculine or feminine), their number (singular, dual or plural), their case (nominative, genitive or accusative), and whether they are definite or indefinite.

CONCRETE VS. ABSTRACT NOUNS

IN ENGLISH

- Concrete nouns used to make general statements are normally plural and without an article.

  Barking *dogs* don't bite.
  Nuts can be dangerous.
  Books are very expensive nowadays.

Occasionally a singular concrete noun is used with the definite article to state a general truth.

  The camel is called "the ship of the desert."
  The dog is man's best friend.
  The book is the basis of our educational system.

- Abstract nouns used to make general statements are normally singular without an article.

  Love is blind.
  Honesty is the best policy.
  Truth is stranger than fiction.

IN ARABIC

- Concrete nouns used to make general statements are normally singular with the definite article.

  ***Camels** [are] useful animals.*
  pl. noun
  'a-l-jamal-u ḥayāwān-u-n nāfiᶜ-u-n. (الجملُ حيوانٌ نافعٌ)
  'a-l- (ال) + sing. nom. noun

- Abstract nouns normally take the definite article, unless followed by a genitive noun.

  'a-l-karam-u (الكرمُ) *generosity*
  'a-l-ṣadāqat-u (الصداقةُ) *friendship*

CAREFUL — To select the correct Arabic form of a concrete noun, you must distinguish in English between a plural noun used to make a general statement from the plural of an indefinite noun.

- if the plural noun is used to make a general statement → the definite article + a plural noun

  ***Books** [are] necessary for education.*

  pl. noun in general statement

  'a-l-kutub-u (الكتُبُ)

  'a-l- (ال) + pl. nom. noun

- if the plural noun is indefinite → a plural noun in the appropriate case + **-n**.

  *Karim brought (**some**) **books** to school.*

  pl. indef. noun

  kutub-a-n (كُتباً)

  noun pl. acc. + **-n**

CHAPTER 7

WHAT IS THE POSSESSIVE?

The term **POSSESSIVE** means that one noun, i.e., the possessor, owns or possesses another noun, i.e., the possessed.

The teacher's book is on the table.
possessor (teacher's) — possessed (book)

IN ENGLISH

There are two constructions to show possession.

1. An apostrophe can be used. In this construction, the possessor comes before the possessed.
   - singular possessor adds an apostrophe + an "s"

     Salman's hat
     a *tree's* branches
     singular possessor

   - plural possessor ending with "s" adds only an apostrophe after the "s"

     the *students'* teacher
     the *girls'* club
     plural possessor

   - plural possessor not ending with "s" adds an apostrophe + "s"

     the *children's* father
     the *men's* mother
     plural possessor

2. The word *of* can be used. In this structure the possessed comes before the possessor.
   - a singular or plural possessor is preceded by *of the* or *of a*

     the book *of the* professor
     the branches *of a* tree
     singular possessor

     the teacher *of the* students
     plural possessor

IN ARABIC

In Arabic, the structure to express possession parallels the "of" construction (2 above). The possessor is always in the genitive case, but possession is expressed differently depending on whether the possessed noun is definite or indefinite (see *What is an Article?*, p. 25).

Definite possessed noun — The noun possessed in the appropriate case + the definite or indefinite noun possessor in the genitive case. In this construction the noun possessed is automatically made definite, without the need for a definite article, by the genitive noun that follows. This construction, called the **genitive construct** or **idāfa** (إضافة)(from the Arabic **'iḍāfatun**(إضافةٌ) "annexation"), is the normal construction to show possession (see p. 23 in *What is Meant by Case?* for additional uses of the genitive construct).

*the teacher **of the** students (the students' teacher)*
muᶜallim-u -l-ṭullāb-**i** (معلمُ الطلابِ)

possessed	possessor
def.	def.
nom. sing.	gen. pl.

*the book **of a** professor (a professor's book)*
kitāb-u 'ustā<u>dh</u>-**i-n** (كتابُ أستاذٍ)

possessed	possessor
def.	indef.
nom. sing.	gen. sing.

*in **the** book **of** Salim (Salim's book)*
fī kitāb-i salīm-**i-n** (في كتاب سليمٍ)

possessed	possessor
def.	def.
gen. sing.	gen. sing.

*I visited **the** house **of a** neighbor (a neighbor's house).*
zur-tu bayt-a jār-**i-n**. (زرتُ بيت جارٍ)

possessed	possessor
def.	indef.
acc. sing.	gen. sing.

Indefinite possessed noun — The noun possessed in the appropriate case + nunation + the preposition **li-**(لِ) *belonging to* + the noun possessor in the genitive case.

***a** teacher **of the** students (a teacher belonging to the students)*
muᶜallim-u-**n li** -**l**-ṭullāb-**i** (معلمٌ للطلابِ)

possessed	possessor
indef.	def.
nom. sing.	gen. pl.

a *book* ***of*** *Salim's (a book belonging to Salim)*
kitāb-u-**n** **li**-salīm-**i-n** (كتابٌ لسليمٍ)

possessed	possessor
indef.	def.
nom. sing.	gen. sing.

in ***a*** *professor's book (in a book belonging to a professor)*
fī kitāb-i-**n** **li**-'ustādh-**i-n** (في كتابٍ لاستاذٍ)

possessed	possessor
indef.	indef.
gen. sing.	gen. sing.

I visited ***a*** *neighbor's house.*
(I visited a house belonging to a neighbor.)
zur-tu bayt-a-**n** **li**-jār-**i-n** (زرتُ بيتاً لجارٍ)

possessed	possessor
indef.	indef.
acc. sing.	gen. sing.

See also *What is Meant by Case?*, p. 20, *What is a Possessive Adjective?*, p. 50 and *What is a Possessive Pronoun?*, p. 68.

CHAPTER

8

WHAT IS A SUBJECT?

In a sentence the person or thing that performs the action of the verb is called the **SUBJECT**.

To find the subject of a sentence always look for the verb first, then ask, *who?* or *what?* before the verb (see *What is a Verb?*, p. 84). The answer will be the subject.[1]

> Muna speaks Arabic.
>
> VERB: speaks
>
> Who speaks Arabic? ANSWER: Muna.
>
> The subject refers to one person; it is singular.
>
> Muna's books cost a lot of money.
>
> VERB: cost
>
> What costs a lot of money? ANSWER: books.
>
> The subject refers to more than one thing; it is plural.

If a verb has more than one subject, the subject is considered plural (see *What is Meant by Number?*, p. 16).

> The book and the pencil are on the table.
>
> VERB: are
>
> What is on the table? ANSWER: the book and the pencil.
>
> The subject refers to more than one thing; it is plural.

If a sentence has more than one verb, you have to find the subject of each verb.

> The boys were cooking while Zaynab set the table.
>
> VERBS: were, set
>
> *Boys* is the plural subject of *were.*
>
> *Zaynab* is the singular subject of *set.*

IN ENGLISH

Always ask *who?* or *what?* before the verb to find the subject. Never assume that the first word in the sentence is the subject. Subjects can be located in several different places, as you can see in the following examples (the subject is in **boldface** and the verb is *italicized*).

> *Did* **the game** *start* on time?
>
> After playing for two hours, **Jamil** *was* exhausted.
>
> Jihan's **brothers** *arrived* yesterday.

[1]The subject performs the action in an active sentence, but is acted upon in a passive sentence (see *What is Meant by Active and Passive Voice?*, p. 123).

IN ARABIC

In Arabic sentences with a verb (see p. 34 for Arabic verbless sentences), the subject is identified the same way as it is in English. Unlike English, which uses an independent pronoun for the subject, in Arabic the subject is indicated by the ending of the verb (see *What is a Verb Conjugation?*, p. 90).

'akal-**a**(أكلَ)
ate ***he*** → *he ate*

'akal-**ū** (أكلوا)
ate ***they*** → *they ate*

Whereas in English a verb always agrees with the subject regardless of where the subject is placed in a sentence, in Arabic the singular form of the verb is used, regardless of the number of the subject, if the verb precedes the subject.

*The professors **arrived** and **ate** at the restaurant.*
waṣal-a -l-'asātidhat-u wa-**'akal-ū** fī -l-maṭᶜam-i.
(وصل الأساتذة وأكلوا في المطعمِ)

- **waṣala** (وصلَ)*(he) arrived*: verb, 3rd pers. masc., verb precedes subj. → sing., perfect
- **-l-'asātidhatu** (الاساتذة) *the professors*: noun, masc. pl. def., subj. of **waṣala**(وصلَ) → nom.
- **wa**(و)- *and*: conjunction
- **'akalū** (أكلوا) *(they) ate:* verb, 3rd pers. masc., subj. precedes verb → pl., perfect
- **fī** (في) *in:* preposition
- **-l-maṭᶜami** (المطعم) *the restaurant*: noun, masc. sing. def., obj. of **fī** (في) → gen.

*And **the students** arrived also.*
wa-l-ṭullāb-u waṣal-ū 'ayḍan. (والطلاب وصلوا أيضاً)

- **wa**(و)- *and*: conjunction
- **-l-ṭullābu** (الطلاب)*the students*: noun, masc. pl. def., subj. of **waṣalū** (وصلوا) → nom.
- **waṣalū** (وصلوا) *(they) arrived*: verb, 3rd pers. masc. pl., perfect
- **'ayḍan** (أيضًا) *also*: adverb

As different Arabic verb tenses are introduced, you will learn whether the subject is placed before or after the verb and how it affects the form of the verb (see *What is Meant by Tense?*, p. 103).

CHAPTER

9

WHAT IS A PREDICATE WORD?

A **PREDICATE WORD** is a word connected back to the subject by a linking verb. A **LINKING VERB** is a verb that acts like an equal sign.

> Karim is my friend. [Karim = friend]
> subject | predicate word
> linking verb

IN ENGLISH

The most common linking verbs in English are *to be, to seem* and *to become.* The noun, pronoun or adjective that follows a linking verb is called a predicate word (see *What is a Noun?*, p. 11; *What is a Pronoun?*, p. 55, *What is an Adjective?*, p. 40).

> Samira *is* an Iraqi visitor.
> linking verb
> subject → *Samira* = predicate noun → *visitor*

> The winners *are* whoever can answer this question.
> linking verb
> subject → *winners* = predicate pronoun → *whoever*

> Hani *seems* tired.
> linking verb
> subject → *Hani* = predicate adjective → *tired*

IN ARABIC

In Arabic, the form of the predicate word depends on whether the sentence has a verb or not. In Arabic, the verb *to be* in the present tense is not expressed, thereby creating a sentence without a verb; i.e., a **VERBLESS SENTENCE**. All other sentences, called **VERBAL SENTENCES**, have a verb.

VERBLESS SENTENCE — In verbless sentences the predicate word is in the nominative case indefinite (see *What is Meant by Case?*, p. 20, see p. 26 for nunation).

> *Mr. Jamal [is]* ***a professor*** *at the University.*
> 'al-sayyid-u jamāl-u-n **'ustādh-u-n** fī-l-jāmiᶜat-i.
> (السيدُ جمالٌ استاذٌ في الجامعةِ)
>
> • **'al-sayyidu** (السيدُ) *mister*: noun, masc. sing. def., together with **jamālun** (جمالٌ) subj. in verbless sentence → nom.

- **jamālun** (جمالٌ)*Jamal*: proper noun, masc. sing. def., together with **'a-l-sayyidu** (السيدُ) subj. in verbless sentence → nom.
- **'ustādhun** (استاذٌ) *a professor*: noun, masc. sing., predicate → nom. indef.
- **fī** (في) *in*: preposition
- **-l-jāmiʿati** (الجامعةِ) *the university*: noun, fem. sing. def., obj. of **fī** (في) → gen.

VERBAL SENTENCE — In verbal sentences the predicate word is in the accusative case indefinite.

*Jamal was **a professor**.*
kān-a jamāl-u-n **'ustādh-a-n** (كان جمالٌ استاذاً).

- **kāna** (كان) *(he) was*: verb, 3rd pers. mas. sing., perfect
- **jamālun** (جمالٌ) *Jamal*: proper noun, masc. sing. def., subj. of **kāna** (كان) → nom.
- **'ustādhan** (استاذاً) *professor*: noun, masc. sing., predicate of **kāna** (كان)→ acc. indef.

*Wasim seems **sad** today.*
wasīm-u-n yabdū **ḥazīn-a-n** -l-yawm-a. (وسيمٌ يبدو حزيناً اليومَ)

- **wasīmun** (وسيمٌ) *Wasim*: proper noun, masc. sing. def., subj. of **yabdū** (يبدو) → nom.
- **yabdū** (يبدو) *seems*: verb, 3rd pers. masc. sing., imperfect
- **ḥazīnan** (حزيناً) *sad*: adjective, masc. sing., predicate of **yabdū** (يبدو) → acc. indef.
- **-l-yawma** (اليومَ) *today*: noun, masc. sing. def., used as time expression → acc.

*And Jamal will be **dean**.*
wa-sa-yakūn-u jamālu-n **ʿamīd-a-n** (وسيكونُ جمالٌ عميداً).

- **wa**(و)- *and*: conjunction
- **sa** (س) - *will*: future prefix
- **yakūnu** (يكونُ)*(he) will be*: verb, 3rd pers. sing. masc., imperfect
- **jamālun** (جمالٌ) *Jamal*: proper noun, subj. → nom.
- **ʿamīdan** (عميداً) *a dean*: noun, masc. sing., predicate of **sayakūnu** (سيكونُ)→ acc. indef.

CHAPTER
10

WHAT ARE OBJECTS?

An **OBJECT** is a noun or pronoun related to a verb or a preposition. An object of a verb tells us where the action of the verb is directed. An object of a preposition gives information introduced by a preposition.

Ihab writes a *letter*.
verb — object

The boy left with *his father*.
preposition — object

We will study the three types of objects separately: direct object, indirect object and object of a preposition. Since noun and pronoun objects are identified the same way, we have limited the examples in this section to noun objects (for examples with pronoun objects see *What is an Object Pronoun?*, p. 62).

DIRECT AND INDIRECT OBJECTS

IN ENGLISH

The terms "direct" and "indirect" indicate the manner in which the noun or pronoun object is related to the verb. Object words are often referred to as being in the **OBJECTIVE CASE** (see p. 22).[1]

DIRECT OBJECT — A direct object is a noun or pronoun that receives the action of the verb. It answers the one-word question *what*? or *whom?* asked after the verb.

They chose *Nabil.*
They chose whom? ANSWER: Nabil.
Nabil is the direct object.

INDIRECT OBJECT — An indirect object is the noun or pronoun that receives the benefit of the action of the verb through the preposition "to" or "for" (see *What is a Preposition?*, p. 135). Thus, it answers the question *to whom?* or *for whom?* asked after the verb.

[1]In this section, we will consider active sentences only (see *What is Meant by Active and Passive Voice?*, p. 123).

Muhsin wrote *to his mother.*

To whom did Muhsin write? ANSWER: To his mother.

Mother is the indirect object.

The class made this *for their teacher.*

For whom did they make this? ANSWER: For their teacher.

Teacher is the indirect object.

IN ARABIC

As in English, an object receives the action of the verb. Nouns and pronouns serving as direct and indirect objects are in the accusative case (see *What is Meant by Case?*, p. 20).

Have you seen ***the people*** *in the park?*

You saw what? ANSWER: The people → dir. obj. noun

hal ra'ayt-a **–l-nāsa** fī l-ḥadīqat-i? (هل رأيت الناس في الحديقةِ؟)

- **hal**(هل): interrogative particle
- **ra'ayta** (رأيتَ) *you saw:* verb, 2nd pers. masc. sing., perfect
- **–l-nāsa** (النّاسَ) *the people:* noun, masc. pl. def., dir. obj. of **ra'ayta** (رأيتَ)→ acc.
- **fī** (في) *in:* preposition
- **l-ḥadīqati** (الحديقةِ) *the park:* noun, fem. sing. def., obj. of **fī** (في)→ gen.

They gave ***the teacher a gift.***

They gave what? ANSWER: A gift → dir. obj. noun

They gave to whom? ANSWER: The teacher → ind. obj. noun

'aʿṭa-w **-l-muʿallimat-a hadiyyat-a-n.**(أعطوا المعلمةَ هديةً)

- **'aʿṭaw** (أعطوا) *they gave:* verb, 3rd pers. masc. pl., perfect
- **-l-muʿallimata** (المعلمةَ) *the teacher:* noun, fem. sing. def., ind. obj. of **'aʿṭaw** (أعطوا)→ acc.
- **hadiyyatan** (هديةً) *a gift:* noun, fem. sing. indef., dir. obj. of **'aʿṭaw** (أعطوا)→ acc.

SENTENCES WITH A DIRECT AND AN INDIRECT OBJECT

IN ENGLISH

When a sentence has two different objects, a direct and an indirect object, there are two possible constructions.

- subject (S) + verb (V) + direct object (DO) + *to* + indirect object (IO)

They gave *flowers to the teacher.*
S V DO IO

Who gave flowers? They.

They is the subject.

They gave *what?* Flowers.

Flowers is the direct object.

They gave flowers *to whom?* The teacher.

The teacher is the indirect object.

- subject + verb + indirect object + direct object

  They gave *the teacher flowers.*
  S V IO DO

  Who gave flowers? They.
  They is the subject.

  They gave *what?* Flowers.
  Flowers is the direct object.

  They gave flowers *to whom?* The teacher.
  The teacher is the indirect object.

In either construction, the function of the words in these two sentences is the same because they answer the same question. Be sure to ask the questions to establish the function of words in a sentence.

IN ARABIC

Like English, Arabic has two possible constructions.

- verb (V) + subject (S) + indirect object (IO) in accusative + direct object (DO) in accusative case

  Nabil gave ***Tariq the letter***.
  S V IO DO

  Nabil gave what? ANSWER: the letter.
  The letter → direct object → accusative

  He gave it to whom? ANSWER: To Tariq.
  Tariq → indirect object → accusative

  'aᶜṭā nabīl-u-n **ṭāriq-a-n -l-risālat-a** (أعطى نبيلٌ طارقاً الرسالةَ).
  - **'aᶜṭā** (أعْطى) *(he) gave):* verb, 3rd pers. masc. sing., perfect
  - **nabīlun** (نبيلٌ) *Nabil*: proper noun, masc. sing. def., subj. of **'aᶜṭā** (أعْطى) → nom.
  - **ṭāriqan** (طارقاً) *Tariq:* proper noun, masc. sing. def., indir. obj. of **'aᶜṭā** (أعْطى) → acc.
  - **-l-risālata** (الرسالةَ) *the letter:* noun, fem. sing. def., dir. obj. of **'aᶜṭā** (أعْطى) → acc.

- verb (V) + subject (S) + direct object (DO) in accusative case + **li-** (لِ) (preposition) + indirect object (IO) now an object of preposition in genitive case

  Nabil gave ***the letter to Tariq.***
  S V DO IO

  'aᶜṭā nabīl-u-n **-l-risālat-a li-ṭāriq-i-n** (أعطى نبيلٌ الرسالةَ لطارقٍ).
  - **'aᶜṭā** (أعْطى) *(he) gave:* verb, 3rd pers. masc. sing., perfect
  - **nabīlun** (نبيلٌ) *Nabil*: proper noun, masc. sing. def., subj. of **'aᶜṭā** (أعْطى) → nom.
  - **-l-risālata** (الرسالةَ) *the letter:* noun, fem. sing. def., dir. obj. of **'aᶜṭā** (أعْطى) → acc.
  - **li** (لِ)- *to:* preposition
  - **ṭāriqin** (طارقٍ) *Tariq:* proper noun, masc. sing. def., obj. of **li** (لِ) → gen.

Your textbook or dictionary will indicate which object pattern or patterns particular verbs may take.

OBJECT OF A PREPOSITION

IN ENGLISH

An object of a preposition is a noun or pronoun that follows a preposition and is related to it. It answers the question *whom?* or *what?* asked after the preposition.

Khalil is *in church.*

Khalil is *in what?* In church.

Church is the object of the preposition *in.*

He went *with Karim.*

He went *with whom?* With Karim.

Karim is the object of the preposition *with.*

IN ARABIC

In Arabic nouns and pronouns serving as objects of prepositions are in the genitive case.

ʼilā **-l-qāhirat-i** (إلى القاهرةِ)

obj. of prep. **ʼilā** (إلى) *to* → gen.
*to **Cairo***

ʿalā **-l-ṭāwilat-i** (على الطاولةِ)

obj. of prep. **ʿalā** (على)*on* → gen.
*on the **table***

baʿda **-l-ṣaff-i** (بعد الصفِ)

obj. of prep. **baʿda** (بعد) *after* → gen.
*after **class***

CHAPTER

11

WHAT IS AN ADJECTIVE?

An **ADJECTIVE** is a word that describes a noun or a pronoun. There are different types of adjectives that are classified according to the way they describe a noun or pronoun.

DESCRIPTIVE ADJECTIVE — A descriptive adjective indicates a quality of someone or something (see p. 42).

> Amjad lived in a *large* house.
> Stars in the desert are *bright*.

POSSESSIVE ADJECTIVE— A possessive adjective shows who possesses someone or something (see p. 50).

> Najib lost *his* ticket to the concert.
> She never wrote *her* family.

INTERROGATIVE ADJECTIVE — An interrogative adjective asks a question about someone or something (see p. 52).

> *What* lesson are we on now?
> *Which* shirt did you choose?

DEMONSTRATIVE ADJECTIVE — A demonstrative adjective points out someone or something (see p. 54).

> I couldn't understand *this* question.
> *That* senator visited Baghdad last week.

IN ENGLISH

English adjectives usually do not change their form, regardless of the noun or pronoun described.

IN ARABIC

Like English, Arabic has descriptive adjectives; however, Arabic uses pronouns instead of possessive, interrogative and demonstrative adjectives. In the following chapters you will see how Arabic adjectives change form to reflect gender (see *What is Meant by Gender?*, p. 13). For number, case and definiteness, they follow the same rules as nouns (see *What is Meant by Number?*, p. 16, *What is Meant by Case?*, p. 20 and *What is an Article?*, p. 25). Adjectives may also be changed to show degree (*What is Meant by Comparison of Adjectives?*, p. 45).

The dictionary form of an adjective is masculine, singular, nominative, indefinite.

kabīr-u-n (كبيرٌ) *big*

- kabīr — stem: masc. sing.
- -u — case: nom.
- -n — indefinite: nunation

CHAPTER 12

WHAT IS A DESCRIPTIVE ADJECTIVE?

A **DESCRIPTIVE ADJECTIVE** is a word that indicates a quality of a noun or pronoun. As the name implies, it describes the noun or pronoun.

The book is *interesting.*

noun described	descriptive adjective

IN ENGLISH

A descriptive adjective does not change form, regardless of the noun or pronoun it modifies.

The students are *intelligent.*
She is an *intelligent* person.

The adjective *intelligent* is the same although the persons described are different in number (*students* is plural and *person* is singular).

Descriptive adjectives are divided into two groups depending on how they are connected to the noun they modify.

ATTRIBUTIVE ADJECTIVE — An attributive adjective is connected directly to the noun it describes and always precedes it.

She lived in a *large* house.

attributive adjective	noun described

They have a *kind* teacher.

attributive adjective	noun described

PREDICATE ADJECTIVE — A predicate adjective is connected to the noun it describes, always the subject of the sentence, by **LINKING VERBS** such as *to be, to feel, to look.*

The teacher seems *kind.*

noun described	linking verb	predicate adjective

The house appears *large.*

noun described | linking verb | predicate adjective

IN ARABIC

As in English, descriptive adjectives can be identified as attributive or predicate adjectives according to the way they are connected to the noun they describe. Unlike English, however, where descriptive adjectives never change form, all Arabic descriptive adjectives agree with the noun they modify; that is, they change form in order to match the gender, number, case and definiteness of the noun.

*the **big** book*
'al-kitāb-**u** -l-kabīr-**u** (الكتابُ الكبيرُ)
- **'al-kitābu** (الكتابُ) *the book:* noun, masc. sing. nom. def.
- **-l-kabīru** (الكبيرُ) *the big:* adjective, masc. sing. nom. def.

*a **big** city*
madīn**at-u-n** kabī**rat-u-n** (مدينةٌ كبيرةٌ)
- **madīnatun** (مدينةٌ) *a city:* noun, fem. sing. nom. indef.
- **kabīratun** (كبيرةٌ) *big:* adjective, fem. sing. nom. indef.

Attributive adjective — Unlike English attributive adjectives that precede the noun described, Arabic attributive adjectives follow the noun described.

*a **new** student*
ṭālibat-u-n **jadīdat-u-n** (طالبةٌ جديدةٌ)
- **ṭālibatun** (طالبةٌ) *a student:* noun, fem. sing. nom. indef.
- **jadīdatun** (جديدةٌ) *new:* attributive adjective, agrees with **ṭālibatun** (طالبةٌ) → fem. sing. nom. indef.

*with **the new** student*
maᶜa -l-ṭālibat-i **-l-jadīdat-i** (مع الطالبةِ الجديدةِ)
- **maᶜa** (مع) *with:* preposition
- **-l-ṭālibati** (الطالبةِ) *the student:* noun, fem. sing. def., obj. of **maᶜa** (مع) → gen.
- **-l-jadīdati** (الجديدةِ) *new:* attributive adjective, agrees with **-l-ṭālibati** (الطالبةِ) → fem. sing. def. gen.

*with **the new** students*
maᶜa -l-ṭālibāt-i **-l-jadīdāt-i** (مع الطالباتِ الجديداتِ)
- **maᶜa** (مع) *with:* preposition
- **-l-ṭālibāti** (الطالباتِ) *the students:* noun, fem. pl. def., obj. of **maᶜa** (مع) → gen.
- **-l-jadīdāti** (الجديداتِ) *new:* attributive adjective, agrees with **-l-ṭālibāti** (الطالباتِ) → fem. pl. def. gen.

PREDICATE ADJECTIVE — Although predicate adjectives agree with the subject in gender and number, they are always indefinite. Their case depends on whether they are in a verbless sentence or not (see *What is a Predicate Word?*, p. 34).

- in a verbless sentence → nominative case

  This student [is] ***new.***
  hādhihi -l-ṭālibat-u **jadīdat-u-n.** (هذهِ الطالبةُ جديدةٌ)
  - **hādhihi** (هذهِ) *this:* demonstrative pronoun, agrees with **-l-ṭālibatu** (الطالبةُ) → fem. sing. nom.
  - **-l-ṭālibatu** (الطالبةُ) *the student:* noun, fem. sing. def., subj. in verbless sentence → nom.
  - **jadīdatun** (جديدةٌ) *new:* adjective, agrees with **-l-ṭālibatu** (الطالبةُ)→ fem. sing., predicate → nom. indef.

- in a sentence with a linking verb → accusative case

  The problem ***was difficult.***
  kān-at -l-mushkilat-u **ṣaʿbat-a-n** (كانت المشكلةُ صعبةً).
  - **kānat** (كانت) *(she) was:* verb, 3rd pers. fem. sing., perfect
  - **-l-mushkilatu** (المشكلةُ) *the problem:* noun, fem. sing. def., subj. of **kānat** (كانت) → nom.
  - **ṣaʿbatan** (صعبةً) *difficult:* adjective, agrees with **-l-mushkilatu** (المشكلةُ) → fem. sing., predicate of **kānat**(كانت)→ acc. indef.

Your textbook will introduce you to different types of descriptive adjective and how they are formed.

CHAPTER 13

WHAT IS MEANT BY COMPARISON OF ADJECTIVES?

The term COMPARISON OF ADJECTIVES is used when two or more persons or things have the same quality indicated by a descriptive adjective and we want to show which of these persons or things has a greater, lesser, or equal degree of that quality.

comparison of adjectives

The moon is *bright* but the sun is *brighter.*

adjective modifies *moon* — adjective modifies *sun*

Both nouns, moon and sun, have the same quality indicated by the adjective *bright,* and we want to show that the sun has a greater degree of that quality (i.e., it is *brighter* than the moon).

In English and in Arabic there are three degrees of comparison: positive, comparative and superlative.

IN ENGLISH

Let's go over the three degrees of comparison:

POSITIVE DEGREE — This form refers to the quality of a person or thing. It is simply the basic adjective form (see *What is a Descriptive Adjective?*, p. 42).

This philosopher is *wise.*
The sword is *expensive.*
His speech was *interesting.*

COMPARATIVE DEGREE — This form compares the quality of one person or thing with that of another person or thing or a group of persons or things. The comparison can indicate that one or the other has more, less, or the same amount of that quality. It is formed differently depending on the length of the adjective.

- short adjective + *-er* + *than*

  This philosopher is *wiser than* most men.
  The sun is *brighter than* the moon.

- *more* + longer adjective + *than*

  The sword is *more expensive than* the shield.
  This book is *more interesting than* that one.

Superlative degree — This form is used to stress the highest degree of a quality. It is formed differently depending on the length of the adjective.

- *the* + short adjective + *-est*

  This philosopher is *the wisest* in the Middle East.
  The sun is *the brightest* star in our heavens.

- *the most* + longer adjective

  This sword is *the most expensive* in Damascus.
  This will be *the most important* exam of the year.

IN ARABIC

As in English, Arabic adjectives can express three degrees of comparison.

Positive degree — This form is expressed by the dictionary form of the adjective which agrees in gender and number with the noun it modifies.

Adil [is] ***tall.***
ʿādil-u-n **ṭawīl-u-n** (عادلٌ طويلٌ) .

- **ʿādilun** (عادلٌ) *Adil:* proper noun, masc. sing. def., subj. in verbless sentence → nom.
- **ṭawīlun** (طويلٌ) *tall:* predicate adjective, agrees with **ʿādilun** (عادلٌ) → masc. sing., predicate → nom. indef.

That [is] a ***good*** *idea.*
hā<u>dh</u>ihi fikrat-u-n **jayyidat-u-n** (هذه فكرةٌ جيدةٌ).

- **hā<u>dh</u>ihi** (هذه) *this*: demonstrative pronoun, agrees with **fikratun** (فكرةٌ) → fem. sing., subj. in verbless sentence → nom.
- **fikratun** (فكرةٌ) *idea:* noun, fem. sing., predicate → nom. indef.
- **jayyidatun** (جيدةٌ) *good*: attributive adjective, agrees with **fikratun** (فكرةٌ) → fem. sing. nom. indef.

Rami is reading an ***interesting*** *book.*
rāmī yaqra'-u kitāb-a-n **mu<u>sh</u>awwiq-a-n** (رامي يقرأ كتاباً مشوِّقاً).

- **rāmī** (رامي) *Rami:* proper noun, masc. sing. def., subj. of **yaqra'u** (يقرأ) → nom.
- **yaqra'u** (يقرأ) *is reading:* verb, 3rd pers. masc. sing., imperfect
- **kitāban** (كتاباً) *a book:* noun, masc. sing. indef., dir. obj. of **yaqra'u** (يقرأ) → acc.
- **mu<u>sh</u>awwiqan** (مشوِّقاً) *interesting:* attributive adjective, agrees with **kitāban** (كتاباً) → masc. sing., acc. indef.

In Arabic the comparative and superlative degrees are expressed by a special pattern, **'aCCaCu**, called the **elative pattern.** The final **-u** of the pattern identifies it as one of those nouns and adjectives that take the two-case declension: **-u** (nom.) and **-a** (gen./acc.) when it is indefinite and the three-case declension: **-u** (nom.), **-i** (gen.), **-a** (acc.) when it is definite. The elative never takes nunation, whether it is definite or indefinite. Comparative degree is expressed by an indefinite elative and the superlative by a definite elative. In both instances the form of the elative is masculine singular, regardless of the gender and number of the word modified, and takes its case from its function in the sentence.

COMPARATIVE DEGREE — This degree is expressed with the indefinite elative form. Below are examples of adjectives changed from the positive to the comparative degree. Note that while the positive word patterns vary, all the adjective stems contain three consonants.

Positive	**Comparative** 'aCCaCu	
kabīr-u-n (كبيرٌ)	**'akbar-u** (أكبرُ)	*big, bigger*
ṭawīl-u-n (طويلٌ)	**'aṭwal-u** (أطولُ)	*tall, taller*
ḥasan-u-n (حسنٌ)	**'aḥsan-u** (أحسنُ)	*good, better*
ṣaᶜb-u-n (صعبٌ)	**'aṣᶜab-u** (أصعبُ)	*difficult, more difficult*

The quality of the person or thing to which the item is compared is introduced by the preposition **min** (من) *from; than.* As such, it is an object of a preposition and requires the genitive case.

Adil [is] ***taller than*** *Ramiz.*
ᶜādil-u-n **'aṭwal-u min** rāmiz-i-n (عادلٌ أطولُ من رامزٍ).

- **ᶜādilun** (عادلٌ) *Adil:* proper noun, masc. sing. def., subj. in verbless sentence → nom.
- **'aṭwalu** (أطولُ) *taller:* elative adjective, masc. sing. indef., predicate → nom.
- **min** (من) *from:* preposition
- **rāmizin** (رامزٍ) *Ramiz:* proper noun, masc. sing. def., obj. of **min** (من) → gen.

Hiyam has gotten ***taller than*** *Sami.*
la-qad 'aṣbaḥ-at hiyām-u **'aṭwal-a min** sāmī. (لقد أصبحت هِيامُ اطولَ من سامي)

- **la**(لـ)- *indeed:* emphatic particle
- **qad**(قد): perfective particle
- **'aṣbaḥat** (أصبحت) *(she) became:* verb, 3rd fem. sing., perfect
- **hiyāmu** (هيامُ) *Hiyam:* proper noun, fem. sing. def., subj. of **'aṣbaḥat** (أصبحت) → nom.
- **'aṭwala** (أطولَ) *taller:* elative adjective, masc. sing. indef., predicate of **'aṣbaḥat** (أصبحت) → acc.
- **min** (من) *from:* preposition
- **sāmī** (سامي) *Sami:* proper noun, masc. sing. def., obj. of **min** (من) → gen.

*I read that in **more than** one article.*
qara't-u <u>dh</u>ālika fī **'ak<u>th</u>ar-a** min maqālat-i-n.(قرأتُ ذلك في اكثرَ من مقالةٍ)

- **qara'tu** (قرأتُ) *I read:* verb, 1st pers. sing., perfect
- **<u>dh</u>ālika** (ذلك) *that:* demonstrative pronoun, no antecedent → masc. sing. def., obj. of **qara'tu** (قرأتُ) → acc.
- **fī** (في) *in:* preposition
- **'ak<u>th</u>ara** (أكثرَ) *more:* elative adjective, masc. sing. indef., obj. of **fī** (في) → gen.
- **min** (من) *from:* preposition
- **maqālatin** (مقالةٍ) *(one) article:* noun, fem. sing. indef., obj. of **min** (من) → gen.

Since the elative pattern is only suited for adjectives of three consonants, the comparative of longer adjectives is expressed with elatives such as **'ak<u>th</u>ar-u** (أكثرُ) *more* or **'aqall-u** (أقلُّ) *less* + the accusative indefinite form of the noun that represents the quality being compared.

*Ramiz [is] **more diligent than** Adil.*
rāmiz-u-n **'ak<u>th</u>ar-u i-jtihād-a-n min** ʿādil-i-n.(رامزٌ اكثرُ اجتهاداً من عادلٍ)

- **rāmizun** (رامزٌ) *Ramiz:* proper noun, masc. sing. def., subj. in verbless sentence → nom.
- **'ak<u>th</u>aru** (اكثرُ) *more:* elative adjective, masc. sing. indef., predicate → nom.
- **i-jtihādan** (اجتهاداً) *as to diligence* (positive: **mujtahidun** (مجتهدٌ) *diligent):* noun, masc. sing., "accusative of respect" [the accusative case indefinite is used for the noun expressing the quality being compared] → acc. indef.
- **min** (من) *than:* preposition
- **ʿādilin** (عادلٍ) *Adil:* proper noun, masc. sing. def., obj. of **min** (من) → gen.

*Her sisters [are] **less diligent than** Adil.*
'a<u>kh</u>awāt-u-hā **'aqall-u -i-jtihād-a-n min** ʿādil-i-n.
(اخواتها اقلُّ اجتهاداً من عادلٍ)

- **'a<u>kh</u>awātu** (اخوات) *sisters:* noun, fem. pl. def., subj. in verbless sentence → nom.
- **-hā** (ها) *her:* suffixed pronoun, 2nd term in gen. construct → gen.
- **'aqallu** (اقلُّ) *less:* elative adjective, masc. sing. indef., predicate→ nom.
- **-i-jtihādan** (اجتهاداً) *as to diligence:* noun, masc. sing., "accusative of respect," noun expressing the quality being compared → acc. indef.
- **min** (من) *from:* preposition
- **ʿādilin** (عادلٍ) *Adil:* proper noun, masc. sing. def., obj. of **min**(من)→ gen.

*This car [is] **more** useful.*
hā<u>dh</u>ihi -l-sayyārat-u **'akthar-u** <u>kh</u>idmat-a-n.
(هذه السيارةُ أكثرُ خدمةً)

- **hā<u>dh</u>ihi** (هذه) *this:* demonstrative pronoun, agrees with **-l-sayyāratu** (السيارةُ) → fem. sing. def. nom.

- **-l-sayyāratu** (السيارةُ) *car:* noun, fem. sing. def., subj. in verbless sentence → nom.
- **'ak<u>th</u>aru** (أكثرُ) *more:* elative adjective, masc. sing. indef., predicate → nom.
- **<u>kh</u>idmatan** (خدمةً) *as to service:* noun, fem. sing., "accusative of respect" → acc. indef.

Superlative degree — This degree is expressed with the elative form made definite in one of two ways:

- by adding the definite article prefix to the elative

Which of the students [is] ***the tallest?***
'ayy-u -l-ṭullāb-i **-l-'aṭwal-u**? (أيّ الطلاب الأطولُ؟)

- **'ayyu** (أيّ) *which?:* interrogative noun, masc. sing., 1st term in gen. construct → def., subj. in verbless sentence → nom.
- **-l-ṭullābi** (الطلاب) *of the students:* noun, masc. pl. def., 2nd term in gen. construct → gen.
- **-l-'aṭwalu** (الأطول) *the tallest:* elative adjective, masc. sing. def., predicate → nom.

Which city was ***the biggest?***
'ayy-u madīnat-i-n kān-at **-l-'akbar-a**? (أي مدينةٍ كانت الأكبرَ؟)

- **'ayyu** (أيّ) *which?:* interrogative noun, masc. sing., 1st term in gen. construct → def., subj. of **kānat** (كانت) → nom.
- **madīnatin** (مدينةٍ) *city:* noun, fem. sing. indef., 2nd term in gen. construct → gen.
- **kānat** (كانت) *(she) was:* verb, 3rd pers. fem. sing., perfect
- **-l-'akbara** (الأكبرَ) *the biggest:* elative adjective, masc. sing. def., predicate → acc.

- by following the elative with a noun or pronoun in the genitive case, thus creating a genitive construct. The genitive construct automatically makes the elative definite, without the need for a definite article (see p. 30 in *What is the Possessive?*).

Who was ***the best student?***
man kāna **'aḥsan-a ṭālib-i-n**? (من كان احسنَ طالبٍ؟)

- **man** (من) *who?:* interrogative pronoun, sing. indef., subj. of **kāna** (كان)
- **kāna** (كان) *(he) was:* verb, 3rd pers. masc. sing., perfect
- **'aḥsana** (احسنَ) *(the) best:* elative adjective, masc. sing., 1st term of gen. construct → def., predicate of **kāna** (كان) → acc.
- **ṭālibin** (طالبٍ) *student:* noun, masc. sing. indef., 2nd term in gen. construct → gen.

CHAPTER

14

WHAT IS A POSSESSIVE ADJECTIVE?

A **POSSESSIVE ADJECTIVE** is a word that describes a noun by showing who possesses that noun.

Whose house is that? It's *his* house.
|
possessive adjective

His shows who possesses the noun *house.* The possessor is "he." The thing possessed is *house.*

IN ENGLISH

Like subject pronouns, possessive adjectives are identified according to the person they represent (see "person," p. 57).

SINGULAR POSSESSOR		
1ST PERSON		my
2ND PERSON		your
3RD PERSON	**(masc.)**	his
	(fem.)	her
	(neuter)	its
PLURAL POSSESSOR		
1ST PERSON		our
2ND PERSON		your
3RD PERSON		their

In the following paragraph possessive adjectives and the things possessed are in *italics.*

We decided to do *our homework* together. Suheila brought *her books*, but Ali forgot *his assignment.* Nasir and Tariq brought a thermos of coffee, but *its lid* was loose and it had all spilled out into *their tote bag.*

IN ARABIC

Arabic has no possessive adjectives. Instead, Arabic uses pronouns referred to as "suffixed pronouns" because they are suffixes attached to the possessed noun. To show possession, a pronoun in the genitive case is suffixed to the possessed noun, as the 2nd term in a genitive construct (see pp. 30 in *What is the Possessive?*).

Here is a list of the genitive case form of suffixed pronouns.

SINGULAR			
1ST PERSON		-ī (ي)	*my*
2ND PERSON	(masc.)	-ka (كَ)	*your*
	(fem.)	-ki (كِ)	*your*
3RD PERSON	(masc.)	-hu (هُ)	*his, its*
	(fem.)	-hā (ها)	*her, its*
DUAL			
2ND PERSON		–kumā (كُما)	*your*
3RD PERSON		–humā (هُما)	*their*
PLURAL			
1ST PERSON		-nā (نا)	*our*
2ND PERSON	(masc.)	-kum (كُم)	*your*
	(fem.)	-kunna (كُنَّ)	*your*
3RD PERSON	(masc.)	-hum (هُم)	*their*
	(fem.)	-hunna (هُنَّ)	*their*

The same genitive case forms of suffixed forms are used for pronouns objects of a preposition. Except for the 1st person singular, the accusative case forms of suffixed pronouns used for direct and indirect objects are the same as the ones above (see *What is an Object Pronoun?*, p. 62).

Here are two examples.

*They took **my book.***
'a<u>kh</u>a<u>dh</u>-ū **kitāb-ī**.(اخذوا كتابي)

- **'a<u>kh</u>a<u>dh</u>ū** (أخذوا) *they took*: verb, 3rd pers. masc. pl., perfect
- **kitāb** (كتاب) **(a)** *book*: noun, masc. sing., 1st term in gen. construct → def., dir. obj. of **'a<u>kh</u>a<u>dh</u>ū** (أخذوا) → acc. [**kitāba** (كتاب) + **-ī** (ي) → **kitābī** (كتابي)]
- **-ī** (ي)*my:* suffixed pronoun, 1st pers. sing., 2nd term in gen. construct → gen. → possessive

*Where [is] **your book?***
'ayna **kitābu-ki** (اين كتابُكِ؟)?

- **'ayna** (اين) *where?:* interrogative adverb
- **kitābu** (كتابُ) *book*: noun, masc. sing., 1st term of gen. construct → def., subj. in verbless sentence → nom.
- **-ki** (كِ) *your:* suffixed pronoun, 2nd pers. fem. sing., 2nd term in gen. construct → gen.

CAREFUL — There are many Arabic equivalents for the pronoun *you;* see pp. 58-9 for the steps to follow to choose the proper Arabic equivalent.

CHAPTER

15

WHAT IS AN INTERROGATIVE ADJECTIVE?

An **INTERROGATIVE ADJECTIVE** is a word that asks for information about a noun.

> *Which* book do you want?
>
> asks information about the noun *book*

IN ENGLISH

The words *which* and *what* are interrogative adjectives when they come in front of a noun and are used to ask a question about that noun.

> *Which* instructor is teaching the course?
> *What* courses are you taking?
> *Whose* book is on the table?

IN ARABIC

Arabic has no interrogative adjectives. Instead, Arabic uses interrogative nouns or interrogative pronouns in the genitive construct (see pp. 23, 30).

- *which?* and *what?*— the interrogative noun **'ayy-un** (أيٌّ) [lit. *which of...? what of...?*] in the appropriate case + modified noun in the genitive; this combination constitutes a genitive construct. Depending on the number of the following noun, **'ayy-un** (أيٌّ) is singular, dual or plural.

Which athletes trained in America?
'ayy-u -l-lāᶜib-īna tadarrab-ū fī 'amrīkā? (ايُّ اللاعبين تدربوا في امريكا؟)

- **'ayyu** (ايُّ) *which?:* interrogative noun, masc. pl., subj. of **tadarrabū** (تدربوا)→ nom.
- **-l-lāᶜibīna** (اللاعبين) *of the athletes*: noun, masc. pl. def., 2nd term in gen. construct → gen.
- **tadarrabū** (تدربوا)*(they) trained:* verb, 3rd pers. masc. pl., perfect
- **fī** (في) *in:* preposition
- **'amrīkā** (امريكا) *America:* proper noun, fem. sing. def., obj. of **fī** (في) → gen.

*To **what** page?*
'ilā **'ayy-i** ṣafḥ**at-i-n** (إلى أي صفحةٍ؟)?

- **'ilā** (إلى) *to:* preposition
- **'ayyi** (أي) *which?*: interrogative noun, masc. sing., obj. of **'ilā** (إلى) → gen.
- **ṣafḥatin** (صفحةٍ) *page:* noun, fem. sing. indef., 2nd term in gen. construct → gen.

- *whose?* — the modified noun in the appropriate case + interrogative pronoun **man?**(من؟) [lit. *of whom?]* in genitive case; this combination constitutes a genitive construct.

***Whose** book [is] this?*

modified noun

kitāb-u **man** hādhā (كتابُ من هذا؟)?

- **kitābu** (كتابُ) *the book:* noun, masc. sing. def., subj. in verbless sentence → nom.
- **man** (من) *whose [of whom]?*: interrogative noun, masc. sing. def., 2nd term in gen. construct → gen.
- **hādhā** (هذا) *this:* demonstrative pronoun, masc. sing., predicate → nom.

***Whose** book did you write in?*
*In the book **of whom** did you write?*
fī kitāb-i **man** katab-ta (في كتابِ مَن كتبتَ؟)?

- **fī** (في) *in:* preposition
- **kitābi** (كتابِ) *the book*: noun, masc. sing. def., obj. of **fī** (في) → gen.
- **man** (من) *whose [of whom]?*: interrogative noun, masc. sing. def., 2nd term in gen. construct → gen.
- **katabta** (كتبتَ) *you wrote*: verb, 2nd pers. masc. sing., perfect

CHAPTER
16

WHAT IS A DEMONSTRATIVE ADJECTIVE?

A **DEMONSTRATIVE ADJECTIVE** is a word used to point out a noun.

> *This* book is interesting.
> points out the noun *book*

IN ENGLISH

The demonstrative adjectives are *this* and *that* in the singular and *these* and *those* in the plural. They are rare examples of English adjectives agreeing in number with the noun they modify: *this* changes to *these* and *that* changes to *those* when they modify a plural noun.

SINGULAR	PLURAL
this book	*these* books
that man	*those* men

The use of *this* or *that* depends on the distance between the person or thing pointed out in relation to the speaker. *This* and *these* refer to persons or objects next to the speaker; *that* and *those* refer to persons or objects away from the speaker.

> *This* building is the library and *that* building is the lab.
> *This*: close to speaker — *that*: away from speaker

> *These* chairs are okay; *those* chairs are rickety.
> *These*: referring to chairs close by — *those*: referring to chairs at a distance

IN ARABIC

Unlike English, Arabic does not have demonstrative adjectives. In order to point out a noun, Arabic uses the demonstrative pronouns (see pp. 72-6 in *What is a Demonstrative Pronoun?*).

CHAPTER

17

WHAT IS A PRONOUN?

A **PRONOUN** is a word used in place of one or more nouns. It may stand, therefore, for a person, animal, place, thing, event, or idea.

Karim is reading a book. *He* is enjoying *it*.
(*He* — pronoun; *it* — pronoun)

He is a pronoun replacing a person, *Karim*.
It is a pronoun replacing a thing, *book*.

A pronoun is used to refer to someone or something that has already been mentioned. The word that the pronoun replaces or refers to is called the **ANTECEDENT** of the pronoun. In the example above, the pronoun *he* refers to the proper noun *Karim*. *Karim* is the antecedent of the pronoun *he*.

IN ENGLISH

There are different types of pronouns, each serving a different function and following different rules. Listed below are the more important types and the chapters in which they are discussed.

PERSONAL PRONOUNS — These pronouns replace nouns referring to persons or things that have been previously mentioned. A different set of pronouns is often used depending on the pronoun's function in the sentence.

- as subject (see p. 57)

  I go; *they* read; *he* runs; *she* sings.

- as direct object (see p. 36)

  Wadad saw *him* at the concert; they both enjoyed *it*.

- as indirect object (see p. 36)

  Hamid gave *them* a book; he gave *us* flowers.

- as object of a preposition (see p. 39)

  Come with *us* or go with *him*.

REFLEXIVE PRONOUNS — These pronouns refer back to the subject of the sentence (see p. 70).

I cut *myself*. We washed *ourselves*. Huda dressed *herself*.

INTERROGATIVE PRONOUNS — These pronouns are used to ask questions (see p. 65).

Who is that? *What* do you want? *Whom* did you see?

Demonstrative pronouns — These pronouns are used to point out persons or things (see p. 72).

This (one) is expensive. *That (one)* is cheap.

Possessive pronouns — These pronouns are used to show possession (see p. 68).

Whose book is that? *Mine. Yours* is on the table.

Relative pronouns — These pronouns are used to introduce relative clauses (see p. 77).

The man *who* came is very nice.
That is the book *that* you read last summer.

IN ARABIC

As in English, Arabic has different types of pronouns. As in English, pronouns reflect gender, number and case appropriate to their function in the sentence (see *What is Meant by Gender?*, p. 13; *What is Meant by Number?*, p.16 and *What is Meant by Case?*, p. 20).

Arabic pronouns can be expressed in one of two ways: as **independent pronouns,** which are separate words (see *What is a Subject Pronoun?*, p. 57) or as **suffixed pronouns,** which are suffixes added to the end of a verb or preposition (see *What is an Object Pronoun?*, p. 62), or at the end of a noun (see *What is a Possessive Adjective?*, p. 50).

CHAPTER

18

WHAT IS A SUBJECT PRONOUN?

A **SUBJECT PRONOUN** is a pronoun used as a subject of a verb.

He worked while *she* read.
subject pronoun — subject pronoun

Who worked? ANSWER: He.
He is the subject of the verb *worked*.

Who read? ANSWER: She.
She is the subject of the verb *read*.

Subject pronouns are divided into three groups: 1st, 2nd, and 3rd person pronouns. The word **PERSON** in this instance does not necessarily mean a human being; it is a grammatical term which can refer to any pronoun.

IN ENGLISH

When a pronoun is used as a subject, the form of the pronoun is said to be in the **SUBJECTIVE CASE**.

Below is a list of English subject pronouns in the order they are usually presented. In the case of the 3rd person singular, more than one pronoun *(he, she, it)* belongs to the same person.

SINGULAR

1ST PERSON
the person speaking — *I*

2ND PERSON
the person spoken to — *you*
Ihab, do *you* sing folk songs?

3RD PERSON
the person or object spoken about — *he, she, it*

PLURAL

1ST PERSON
the person speaking plus others — *we*
Amal and I are free tonight. *We*'re going out.

2ND PERSON
the persons spoken to — *you*
Ali, Ihab and Nazik, do *you* sing folk songs?

3RD PERSON
the persons or objects spoken about — *they*
Muna and Ali are free tonight. *They*'re going out.

As you can see, all the personal pronouns, except *you*, show whether one person or more than one is involved. For instance, the singular *I* is used by the person speaking to refer to himself or herself and the plural *we* is used by the person speaking to refer to himself or herself plus others.

IN ARABIC

Arabic has a series of **INDEPENDENT PRONOUNS** ("independent" words as opposed to "suffixed pronouns") that exist only in the nominative case.

SINGULAR			
1ST PERSON		'anā (أنا)	*I*
2ND PERSON	(masc.)	'anta (أنتَ)	*you*
	(fem.)	'anti (أنتِ)	*you*
3RD PERSON	(masc.)	huwa (هُوَ)	*he, it*
	(fem.)	hiya (هي)	*she, it*
DUAL			
2ND PERSON		'antumā (انتما)	*you*
3RD PERSON		humā (هُما)	*they*
PLURAL			
1ST PERSON		naḥnu (نحنُ)	*we*
2ND PERSON	(masc.)	'antum (انتُمْ)	*you*
	(fem.)	'antunna (انتُنَّ)	*you*
3RD PERSON	(masc.)	hum (هُم)	*they*
	(fem.)	hunna (هُنَّ)	*they*

The English pronouns *it*, *you* and *they* have more than one Arabic equivalent. Here is how to select the appropriate one:

"YOU" (2nd person singular and plural)

IN ENGLISH

The same pronoun *you* is used to address one or more than one person.

Amal, are *you* coming with me?
Amal and Faris, are *you* coming with me?

The same pronoun is used to address males and females.

Fatima, do *you* have any questions?
Jamal, are *you* coming with us?

IN ARABIC

There are five equivalents for *you* in Arabic, depending on the gender and number of persons addressed.

- to address one person → singular

Husayn, how are you?

you (masc.)
'anta (أنتَ)

***Fadwa**, how are **you**?*

you (fem.)
'anti (أنتِ)

- to address two persons → dual

  ***Huda** and **Salim**, how are **you**?*

  you (2 pers.)
  'antumā (انتما)

- to address three or more persons → plural

  ***Ladies** and **gentlemen**, how are **you** today?*

  you (3+ pers. incl. 1 male) → masc.
  'antum (انتُمْ)

  *Good afternoon, **ladies**, how are **you** today?*

  you (3+ pers. female)
  'antunna (انتُنَّ)

"IT" (3rd person singular)

IN ENGLISH

Whenever you are speaking about one thing or idea, you use the pronoun *it*.

Where is the book? *It* is on the table.
Jamal has an idea. *It* is very interesting.

IN ARABIC

There are two equivalents for *it* in Arabic, depending on the gender of the noun being referred to.

*Where [is] the book? **It** [is] on the table.*
'ayna l-kitāb-u? **huwa** ʿalā -l-ṭāwilat-i(أين الكتابُ؟ هُوَ على الطاولة).

- **'ayna** (أين) *where?:* interrogative adverb
- **-l-kitābu** (الكتابُ) *the book*: noun, masc. sing. def., subj. in verbless sentence → nom.
- **huwa** (هُوَ) *it:* pronoun, agrees with **-l-kitābu** (الكتابُ) → masc. sing. def., subj. in verbless sentence → nom.
- **ʿalā** (على) *on:* preposition
- **-l-ṭāwilati** (الطاولةِ) *the table:* noun, fem. sing. def., obj. of **ʿalā** (على) → gen.

*And the letter? **It** [is] also on the table.*
wa-l-risālat-u? **hiya** ka<u>dh</u>ālika ʿalā -l-ṭāwilat-i.
(والرسالةُ؟ هي كذلك على الطاولة)

- **wa** (و)- *and:* conjunction
- **-l-risālatu** (الرسالةُ) *the letter:* noun, fem. sing. def., subj. → nom.
- **hiya** (هيَ) *it:* pronoun, agrees with **-l-risālatu** (الرسالةُ) → fem. sing. def., subj. in verbless sentence → nom.

- **kadhālika** (كذلك) *likewise:* adverb
- **ʿalā** (على) *on:* preposition
- **-l-ṭāwilati** (الطاولة) *the table:* noun, fem. sing. def., obj. of **ʿalā** (على) → gen.

"THEY" (3rd person plural)

IN ENGLISH

Whenever you are speaking about more than one person or thing, you use the plural pronoun *they.*

Salman and Rashid are students; *they* study a lot.
Where are the books? *They* are on the table.

IN ARABIC

There are several equivalents for *they* in Arabic, depending on whether it refers to persons, things, or animals and on their gender and number.

- two persons or things → dual

Where are ***Leila*** *and* ***the visitor****?* ***They*** *are in the library.*
humā (هُما)

- three or more persons → masculine or feminine plural

Where are ***the women professors****?* ***They*** *are in the office.*
they (fem.)
hunna (هُنَّ)

Where are ***the men professors****?* ***They*** *are in the office.*
they (masc.)
hum (هُم)

- three or more non-humans (animals and things) → feminine singular

Where are ***the books****?* ***They*** *are on the shelves.*
they (fem. sing.)
hiya (هيَ)

Unlike English which requires the use of a subject pronoun, Arabic verbs do not need a subject pronoun since the verb itself indicates the doer of the action (see *What is a Verb Conjugation?*, p. 90). The above independent pronouns have three main functions: 1. as subject in a verbless sentence (see p. 34) 2. as predicate in a verbless sentence and 3. to provide emphasis or focus on the antecedent.

VERBLESS SENTENCE — The independent pronoun is required as subject since there is no verb.

He [is] at home.
huwa fī -l-bayt-i (هو في البيت).
|
pronoun subject

The winner [is] ***you.***
'al-ghālib-u **'anta** (الغالبُ انتَ).
|
pronoun predicate

VERBAL SENTENCE — The independent pronoun is not required since the ending of the verb provides all the information we need about the subject: person, number and gender (see *What is a Verb Conjugation?*, p. 90).

[He] greeted Mahir.
sallam-**a** ʿalā māhir-i-n (سلّمَ على ماهرٍ).
|
3rd pers. masc. sing. → *he*

[They] greeted Dunya.
sallam-**ū** ʿalā dunyā (سلّموا على دنيا).
|
3rd pers. masc. pl. → *they*

EMPHASIS — The independent pronoun may be used to place emphasis on or to focus on the antecedent.

The author did not come, ***I*** *came.*
lam ya'ti -l-kātib-u; 'atay-tu **'anā.** (لم يأتِ الكاتبُ؛ أتيتُ انا)

- **lam** (لم) *did not:* perfect tense negative particle
- **ya'ti** (يأتِ) *(he) come:* verb, 3rd pers. masc. sing., imperfect jussive mood
- **-l-kātibu** (الكاتبُ) *the author:* noun, masc. sing. def., subj. of **ya'ti** (يأتِ) → nom.
- **'ataytu** (أتيتُ) *I came:* verb, 1st pers. sing., perfect
- **'anā** (أنا) *I:* independent pronoun, 1st pers. sing.

CHAPTER

19

WHAT IS AN OBJECT PRONOUN?

An **OBJECT PRONOUN** is a pronoun used as the object of a verb or as the object of a preposition.

They invited *me*.
verb — invited; object — *me*

The boy left with *him*.
preposition — with; object — *him*

Since noun and pronoun objects are identified the same way, we refer you to *What are Objects?*, p. 36 as background.

IN ENGLISH

When a pronoun is used as an object of a verb or of a preposition, the form of the pronoun is said to be in the **OBJECTIVE CASE** (see *What is Meant by Case?*, p. 20).

Most pronouns that function as objects in a sentence are different from the ones used as subjects. Here is a list of the subjective and objective forms of English personal pronouns.

Subjective	Objective
I	me
you	you
he, she, it	him, her, it
we	us
you	you
they	them

As you can see only *you* and *it* have the same forms as subjects and objects.

IN ARABIC

Unlike English where object pronouns are separate words, Arabic object pronouns are suffixes, that is, one or two syllables attached to the end of the verb.

Here is a list of the accusative case forms of suffixed pronouns.

Singular

1st person		-nī (ني)	*me*
2nd person	(masc.)	-ka (كَ)	*you*
	(fem.)	-ki (كِ)	*you*
3rd person	(masc.)	-hu (هُ)	*him, it*
	(fem.)	-hā (ها)	*her, it*

DUAL				
2ND PERSON		-kumā	(كُما)	*you*
3RD PERSON		-humā	(هُما)	*them*
PLURAL				
1ST PERSON		-nā	(نا)	*us*
2ND PERSON	(masc.)	-kum	(كُم)	*you*
	(fem.)	-kunna	(كُنَّ)	*you*
3RD PERSON	(masc.)	-hum	(هُم)	*them*
	(fem.)	-hunna	(هُنَّ)	*them*

Except for the 1st person singular, the accusative case forms of suffixed pronouns are the same as the genitive case forms of suffixed pronouns used to show possession (see p. 51 in *What is a Possessive Adjective?*).

- object of a verb → accusative → **-nī** (ني)

  They visited ***me*** *a couple of days ago.*

  dir. obj. → **-nī** (ني)

  They gave ***me*** *a book.*

  ind. obj. → **-nī** (ني)

- object of a preposition → genitive → **-ī** (ي)

  Did she come ***with me****?*

  obj. of prep. →**maʿa** (ي + مع)+ **-ī** (ي) → **maʿ-ī** (معي)

As you can see, there are several Arabic equivalents for the object pronoun *you*. To choose the proper form you must establish to how many persons the *you* refers.

- one person: singular → one man → **-ka** (كَ) (masc.) or one woman → **-ki** (كِ) (fem.)
- two persons: dual → **-kumā** (كُما)
- three or more persons: plural → men or men and women → **-kum** (كُم) (masc.) or all women → **-kunna** (كُنَّ) (fem.)

Here are some examples

Who visited ***you, Hiyam****?*

fem. sing. obj. of verb → acc. → zār-a-**ki** (زارَكِ)

Who visited ***you, Sameer****?*

masc. sing. obj. of verb → acc. → zār-a-**ka** (زارَكَ)

Who visited ***you, Hiyam*** *and* ***Sameer****?*

masc. dual, obj. of of verb → acc. → zār-a-**kumā** (زاركما)

Who visited ***you, Hiyam*** *and* ***Suhayla?***

fem. dual, obj. of verb → acc. → zār-a-**kumā** (زاركما)

Who visited ***you, Hiyam, Suhayla*** *and* ***Sameer?***

masc. pl., obj. of verb → acc. → zār-a-**kum** (زاركم)

CAREFUL — The pronoun *you* can also be the subject of a verb, in which case it is usually omitted in Arabic (see *What is a Subject Pronoun?*, p. 57). Be sure to analyze its function as a first step before selecting the Arabic equivalent.

CHAPTER

20

WHAT IS AN INTERROGATIVE PRONOUN?

An **INTERROGATIVE PRONOUN** is a word that replaces a noun and introduces a question.

Who is coming to the banquet?
replaces a person

What did you eat at the banquet?
replaces a thing

IN ENGLISH

A different interrogative pronoun is used depending on whether it refers to a person or a thing.

PERSON — The interrogative pronoun to ask about persons has three different forms depending on its function in the sentence.

- subject → *who*

  Who wrote that book?
  subject

- object → *whom?*

  Whom do you know?
  object of verb

  From *whom* did you get the book?
  object of prep. *from*

- possessive → *whose?*

  I found a pen. *Whose* is it?
  replacement of possessor of *pen*

THING — There is one interrogative pronoun to ask about things → *what?*[1]

What is in the closet?
refers to one thing or many things

[1]Do not confuse *what* as an interrogative pronoun with *what* as an interrogative adjective "*What* book is on the table?," see p. 52.

IN ARABIC

Like English, Arabic uses different interrogative pronouns to ask about people and to ask about things.

Person — *who, whom, whose* → **man** (من) ?

Who teaches Arabic?
subject → **man** (من)?

Whom did you see?
object → **man** (من) ?

Arabic also uses an interrogative pronoun (see p. 53) for the English interrogative adjective *whose? [of whom?]* → possessed item + **man**(من)?

***Whose book** did you use?*
interr. adj.
kitāb-a man (كتابَ من)
interr. pron.
possessed item *book*

Thing — *what?* → **mā** (ما)? → subject in a verbless sentence or **mā<u>dh</u>ā** (ماذا) → subject or object of verb

***What** [is] this?*
subject of *is* → verbless sentence in Arabic
mā (ما)

***What** happened, Wisam?*
subject of *happened* → verbal sentence in Arabic
mā<u>dh</u>ā (ماذا)

***What** did you do today?*
object of *did do* → verbal sentence in Arabic
mā<u>dh</u>ā (ماذا)

DANGLING PREPOSITIONS

(see *What is a Preposition?*, p. 135 and p. 39 in *What are Objects?*)

IN ENGLISH

In English it is sometimes difficult to identify the function of pronouns that are objects of a preposition because the pronouns are often separated from the preposition. Consequently, in conversation the interrogative subject pronoun *who* is often used instead of the interrogative object pronoun *whom.*

Who did you speak *to?*
interr. pronoun preposition

Who did you get the book *from?*
interr. pronoun — preposition

When a preposition is separated from its object and placed at the end of a sentence or question it is called a **DANGLING PREPOSITION.**

To establish the function of an interrogative pronoun, you will have to change the structure of the sentence by moving the preposition from the end of the sentence or question and placing it before the interrogative pronoun.

Who are you giving the book *to?*
interr. pronoun — preposition
To whom are you giving the book?
indirect object

Who did you get the book *from?*
From whom did you get the book?
object of the preposition *from*

IN ARABIC

Arabic does not allow for dangling prepositions. The preposition must be placed before the interrogative pronoun.

***Whom** did you go to the movies **with**?*
interr. pronoun — preposition
man (من) — **maʿa** (مع)
***With whom** did you go to the movies?*
maʿa man (مع من) ...
prep. obj. of prep.

***What** did you write the letter **with**?*
interr. pronoun — preposition
mā<u>dh</u>ā (ماذا) — **bi-** (ب)
***With what** did you write the letter?*
bi-mā<u>dh</u>ā (بماذا) ...
prep. obj. of prep.

CHAPTER 21

WHAT IS A POSSESSIVE PRONOUN?

A **POSSESSIVE PRONOUN** is a word that replaces a noun and indicates the possessor of that noun.

> Whose house is that? It's *mine*.
>
> (*mine* — possessive pronoun)
>
> *Mine* replaces the noun *house*, the object possessed, and shows who owns it, "I."

IN ENGLISH

Here is a list of the possessive pronouns:

SINGULAR POSSESSOR

1ST PERSON		mine
2ND PERSON		yours
3RD PERSON	(masc.)	his
	(fem.)	hers
	(neuter)	its

PLURAL POSSESSOR

1ST PERSON	ours
2ND PERSON	yours
3RD PERSON	theirs

IN ARABIC

Unlike English, Arabic has no possessive pronouns. Instead, Arabic uses a structure meaning "belonging to" (*belonging to me → mine, belonging to you → yours*, etc.).

- **li-**(لِ) *belonging to* + any noun

  li-l-walad-i (للولد)
  ***belonging to** the boy [the boy's]*

- **la-**(لَ) + the suffixed genitive pronouns

SINGULAR POSSESSOR

1ST PERSON		lī[1] (لي)	*mine [belonging to me]*
2ND PERSON	(masc.)	la-ka (لَكَ)	*yours*
	(fem.)	la-ki (لَكِ)	*yours*
3RD PERSON	(masc.)	la-hu (لَهُ)	*his, its*
	(fem.)	la-hā (لَها)	*hers, its*

[1] As two vowels cannot follow one another in Arabic the short vowel **-a** in **la-** is deleted before **-ī**.

Dual possessor			
2nd person		la–kumā (لَكُما)	*yours [belonging to you two]*
3rd person		la–hum (لَهُما)	*theirs [belonging to them two]*
Plural possessor			
1st person		la-nā (لَنا)	*ours*
2nd person	(masc.)	la-kum (لَكُم)	*yours*
	(fem.)	la-kunna (لَكُنَّ)	*yours*
3re person	(masc.)	la-hum (لَهُم)	*theirs*
	(fem.)	la-hunna (لَهُنَّ)	*theirs*

The same genitive case forms of suffixed pronouns without **li-** are used for possessive pronouns, see p. 51 in *What is a Possessive Adjective?*.

Here are some examples:

*Whose books [are] these? They [are] **his**.*
li-man hādhihi –l-kutub-u? hiya **la-hu** (لمن هذه الكتبُ؟ هي لهُ).

- **li-man** (لمن) *whose? [belonging to whom?]:* predicate in verbless sentence
- **hādhihi** (هذه) *these:* demonstrative pronoun, agrees with **–l-kutubu** (الكتبُ) → fem. sing. def.
- **–l-kutubu** (الكتبُ) *books:* noun, [non-human plural nouns → fem. sing.] fem. sing. def., subj. in verbless sentence → nom.
- **hiya** (هي) *they:* independent pronoun, refers to **–l-kutubu** (الكتبُ) 3 →rd pers. fem. sing.
- **lahu** (لَهُ) *his [belonging to him]:* predicate

*All these books [are] **theirs**.*
kull-u hādhihi –l-kutub-i **la-hum** (كل هذه الكتب لهم).

- **kullu** (كل) *all:* noun, agrees with **-l-kutubi** (الكتبِ) → fem. sing., 1st term in gen. construct → def., subj. in verbless sentence → nom.
- **hādhihi** (هذه) *these:* demonstrative pronoun, agrees with **–l-kutubi** (الكتبِ) → fem. sing. def.
- **–l-kutubi** (الكتبِ) *books:* noun, [non-human plural nouns → fem. sing.] fem. sing. def., together with **hādhihi** (هذه) 2nd term in gen. construct → gen.
- **la-hum** (لَهُم) *theirs [belonging to them]:* predicate

*Whose [is] that house (over there)? [It is] **Ours**.*
li-man dhālika -l-bayt-u? **la-nā** (لمن ذلك البيتُ؟ لنا).

- **li-man** (لمن) *whose? [belonging to whom?]:* predicate
- **dhālika** (ذلك) *that:* demonstrative pronoun, agrees with **-l-baytu** (البيتُ) → masc. sing. def.
- **-l-baytu** (البيتُ) *the house:* noun, masc. sing. def., subj. in verbless sentence → nom.
- **la-nā** (لَنا) *ours [belonging to us]:* predicate

CHAPTER

22

WHAT IS A REFLEXIVE PRONOUN?

A **REFLEXIVE PRONOUN** is a pronoun object that refers back to the subject of the verb.

Suad looked at *herself* in the mirror.

subject + reflexive pronoun → the same person

IN ENGLISH

Reflexive pronouns end with *-self* in the singular and *-selves* in the plural.

SINGULAR		
1ST PERSON		myself
2ND PERSON		yourself
3RD PERSON	**(masc.)**	himself
	(fem.)	herself
	(neuter)	itself
PLURAL		
1ST PERSON		ourselves
2ND PERSON		yourselves
3RD PERSON		themselves

Reflexive pronouns can have a variety of functions: direct objects, indirect objects and objects of a preposition.

I cut *myself* with the dagger.

dir. obj. of *cut*

You should give *yourself* a present.

indir. obj. of *should give*

They talk too much about *themselves*.

obj. of prep. *about*

IN ARABIC

Like English, Arabic uses the word for *self* to form reflexive pronouns: the feminine singular noun **nafs-u-n** (نفسهنّ) *self* in the appropriate case + a singular suffixed pronoun or its plural form **'anfus-u-n** (أنفسهنّ) *selves* in the appropriate case + a plural suffixed pronoun (see p. 51 in *What is a Possessive Adjective?*).

Singular			
1st person		nafs-ī (نفسي)	*myself*
2nd person	(masc.)	nafs-u-**ka** (نفسكَ)	*yourself*
	(fem.)	nafs-u-**ki** (نفسكِ)	*yourself*
3rd person	(masc.)	nafs-u-**hu** (نفسهُ)	*himself, itself*
	(fem.)	nafs-u-**hā** (نفسها)	*herself, itself*
Plural			
1st person		'anfus-u-**nā** (أنفسنا)	*ourselves*
2nd person	(masc.)	'anfus-u-**kum** (أنفسكم)	*yourselves*
	(fem.)	'anfus-u-**kunna** (أنفسكنّ)	*yourselves*
3rd person	(masc.)	'anfus-u-**hum** (أنفسهم)	*themselves*
	(fem.)	'anfus-u-**hunna** (أنفسهنّ)	*themselves*

The case of **nafs-u** (نفسُ) depends on its function in the sentence.

- as direct object → accusative

  *He wounded **himself** with the dagger.*
  jaraḥ-a **nafs-a-hu** bi -l-khanjar-i (جرحَ نفسهُ بالخنجر) .
  - **jaraḥa** (جرحَ) *he wounded:* verb, 3rd pers. masc. sing., perfect
  - **nafsa** (نفس) *self:* noun, 3rd pers. fem. sing. def., dir. obj. of **jaraḥa** (جرحَ) → acc.
  - **-hu** (هُ) *his:* suffixed pronoun, 3rd masc. sing., 2nd term in gen. construct → gen.
  - **bi-** (بِ) *(by means of) with:* preposition
  - **-l-khanjari** (الخنجر) *the dagger:* noun, masc. sing. def., obj. of **bi** (بِ) - → gen.

- as object of prepositon → genitive

  *She **herself** came to the party.*
  jā'-at bi-**nafs-i-hā** 'ilā-l-ḥaflat-i (جاءت بنفسها إلى الحفلةِ).
  - **jā'at** (جاءت) *she came:* verb, 3rd pers. fem. sing., perfect
  - **bi** (بِ)- *by:* preposition
  - **nafsi** (نفسِ) *self:* noun, fem. sing. def., obj. of **bi** (بِ) - → gen.
  - **-hā** (ها) *her:* suffixed pronoun, 3rd pers. fem. sing., 2nd term gen. construct → gen.
  - **'ilā** (إلى) *to:* preposition
  - **-l-ḥaflati** (الحفلةِ) *the party:* noun, fem. sing. def., obj. of **'ilā** (إلى) → gen.

- for emphasis → nominative

  *He **himself** said that.*
  qāl-a dhālika huwa **nafs-u-hu** (قالَ ذلك هو نفسه).
  - **qāla** (قالَ) *he said:* verb, 3rd pers. masc. sing., perfect
  - **dhālika** (ذلك) *that*: demonstrative pronoun, no antecedent → masc. sing., dir. obj. of **qāla** (قالَ)
  - **huwa** (هو) *he:* independent pronoun, 3rd masc. sing., repeating subj. for emphasis → nom.
  - **nafsu** (نفسُ)- *self:* noun, fem. sing. def., repeating subj. for emphasis → nom.
  - **-hu** (هُ) *his:* suffixed pronoun, 3rd pers. masc. sing., 2nd term in gen. construct → gen.

CHAPTER 23

WHAT IS A DEMONSTRATIVE PRONOUN?

A **DEMONSTRATIVE PRONOUN** is a word that replaces a noun as if pointing to it.

Choose a text. *This one* is hard. *That one* is easy.

antecedent — points to a text — points to another text

In English and Arabic, demonstrative pronouns can be used as subjects or objects.

IN ENGLISH

The singular demonstrative pronouns are *this (one)* and *that (one)*; the plural forms are *these* and *those.*

The distinction between *this* and *that* can be used to contrast one object with another, or to refer to things that are not the same distance away. The speaker uses *this* or *these* for the objects closer to him or her and *that* or *those* for the ones farther away.

Here are two chairs. *This one* is firm; *that one* is soft.

antecedent — singular — singular

"These are my books," says Fuad, "I do not use *those."*

referring to the *books* at hand — referring to the *books* at a distance

IN ARABIC

Like English, Arabic has two demonstrative pronouns, each serving to contrast distance. Unlike English, however, where *this* refers only to closeness to the speaker, the Arabic equivalent **hā<u>dh</u>ā** (هذا) refers to something close to the speaker or to the person spoken to. Similarly, unlike *that* which refers only to distance from the speaker, the Arabic equivalent **<u>dh</u>ālika** (ذٰلِكَ) refers to something far from the speaker and from the person spoken to. Consequently, to choose the correct Arabic equivalent you will have to disregard the English *this* or *that* and determine where the antecedent is situated in relationship to the speaker and the person(s) spoken to.

The Arabic demonstrative pronouns can be used either independently or as part of a phrase.

INDEPENDENT USAGE — When the Arabic demonstrative pronoun is used without a noun, it corresponds in usage to the English demonstrative pronoun. If the antecedent is identified somewhere in the sentence, the demonstrative pronoun agrees with it in gender and number; the case depends on the function of the demonstrative pronoun in the sentence. If the reference is not identified, the masculine singular form is used.

*This [is] George and **that** [is] Laila.*
hā<u>dh</u>ā jōrj wa-**tilka** laylā (هذا جورج وتلك ليلي).

- **hā<u>dh</u>ā** (هذا) *this*: demonstrative pronoun, agrees with **jōrj** (جورج) → masc. sing., subj. → nom.
- **jōrj** (جورج) *George*: proper name, masc. sing. def., predicate, antecedent of **hā<u>dh</u>ā** (هذا)
- **wa** (و) - *and:* conjunction
- **tilka** (تلك) *that:* demonstrative pronoun, agrees with **laylā** (ليلي) → fem. sing., subj. in verbless sentence → nom.
- **laylā** (ليلي) *Laila:* proper name, fem. sing. def., predicate, antecedent of **tilka** (تلك)

*What [is] **this** and what [is] **that**?*
mā **hā<u>dh</u>ā** wa-mā **<u>dh</u>ālika** (ما هذا وما ذلك؟) ?

- **mā** (ما) *what?:* interrogative pronoun, subj.
- **hā<u>dh</u>ā** (هذا) *this*: demonstrative pronoun, no antecedent → masc. sing., predicate
- **wa** (و)- *and:* conjunction
- **mā** (ما) *what?:* interrogative pronoun, subj.
- **<u>dh</u>ālika** (ذلك) *that:* demonstrative pronoun, no antecedent → masc. sing., predicate

DEMONSTRATIVE PHRASE — When the Arabic demonstrative pronoun is used with a noun, it corresponds in usage to the English demonstrative adjective (see *What is a Demonstrative Adjective?*, p. 54). The demonstrative phrase consists of the demonstrative pronoun + the definite article **-l-** + the noun. The demonstrative pronoun agrees with the following noun in gender and number and both go in the same case appropriate for their function.

*Where did you buy **this book**?*
'ayna i-<u>sh</u>taray-ti **hā<u>dh</u>ā -l-kitāb-a** (اين اشتريت هذا الكتاب؟)?

- **'ayna** (أين) *where?:* interrogative adverb
- **i-<u>sh</u>tarayti** (اشتريت) *you bought:* verb, 2nd pers. fem. sing., perfect
- **hā<u>dh</u>ā** (هذا) *this:* demonstrative pronoun, agrees with **-l-kitāba** (الكتاب) → masc. sing. acc.
- **-l-kitāba** (الكتاب) *book:* noun, masc. sing. def., dir. obj. of verb→ acc.

When did ***these (two) letters*** *arrive?*
matā waṣal-at **hāt-āni -l-risālat-āni** (متى وصلت هتان الرسالتان؟) ?
. **matā** (متى) *when?:* interrogative adverb
. **waṣalat** (وصلت) *(she) arrived:* verb, 3rd pers., agrees with subj.'s gender **l-risālat-āni** (الرسالتانِ) → fem., verb precedes subj. → sing., perfect
. **hātāni** (هتانِ) *these (two):* demonstrative pronoun, agrees with **-l-risālat-āni** (الرسالتانِ) → fem. dual, nom.
. **-l-risālat-āni** (الرسالتانِ) *two letters:* noun, fem. dual def., subj. of **waṣalat** (وصلت) → nom.

What came in ***that letter*** *yesterday?*
mā<u>dh</u>ā jā'-a 'amsi fī **tilka l-risālat-i**(ماذا جاء امس في تلك الرسالة؟)?
. **mā<u>dh</u>ā** (ماذا) *what?:* interrogative pronoun, subj. of **jā'a** (جاءَ)
. **jā'a** (جاءَ) *(he) came:* verb, 3rd pers. masc. sing., perfect
. **'amsi** (امسِ) *yesterday:* adverb
. **fī** (في) *in:* preposition
. **tilka** (تلك) *that:* demonstrative pronoun, agrees with **l-risālati** (الرسالةِ) → fem. sing. gen.
. **l-risālati** (الرسالةِ) *letter:* noun, fem. sing. def., obj. of **fī** (في) → gen.

To choose the correct form of the demonstrative pronoun, follow these steps.

1. Location:
   a) antecedent is near the speaker or addressee → **hā<u>dh</u>ā** (هذا)
   b) antecedent is away from both the speaker and addressee → **<u>dh</u>ālika** (ذلِكَ)
2. Gender and number:
   a) if antecedent is mentioned → pronoun agrees with it in gender and number
   b) if no antecedent is mentioned → pronoun masculine singular
3. Case:
   a) pronoun in independent usage → based on its function in the sentence
   b) demonstrative pronoun and noun in demonstrative phrase → based on their function in the sentence

Here is a chart you can use as reference.

	Near speaker or addressee		Far from speaker and addressee	
	hā<u>dh</u>ā (هذا) *this, that, these, those*		**<u>dh</u>ālika** (ذلِكَ) *that, those*	
Antecedent Gender:	Masc.	Fem.	Masc.	Fem.
Number: Singular	hā<u>dh</u>ā (هذا)	hā<u>dh</u>ihi (هذه)	<u>dh</u>ālika (ذلِكَ)	tilka (تلكَ)
Dual				
Nom.	hā<u>dh</u>-āni (هذانِ)	hāt-āni (هاتانِ)		
Gen./Acc.	hā<u>dh</u>-ayni(هذينِ)	hāt-ayni(هاتينِ)		
Plural	hā'ulā'i (هؤلاءِ)		'ulā'ika (ألائكَ)	

*Do you see **that** on the horizon?*
hal tarā **d͟hālika** ᶜalā -l-'ufuq-i (هل ترى ذلك على الأفق؟)?
. **hal** (هل): interrogative particle, changes statement to question
. **tarā** (ترى) *you see,* verb, 2nd pers. masc. sing., imperfect
. **d͟hālika** (ذلِكَ) *that over there [far from speaker and addressee]:* demonstrative pronoun, no antecedent → masc. sing.
. **ᶜalā** (على) *on:* preposition
. **-l-'ufuqi** (الأفق) *the horizon:* noun, masc. sing. def., obj. of **ᶜalā** (على) → gen.

***That** [is] a great idea [of yours].*
hād͟hihi fikrat-u-n mumtāzat-u-n (هذه فكرة ممتازة).
. **hād͟hihi** (هذه) *that [near the person addressed]:* demonstrative pronoun, agrees with antecedent **fikratun** (فكرةٌ) → fem. sing., subj. → nom.
. **fikratun** (فكرةٌ) *idea:* noun, fem. sing. indef., predicate in verbless sentence → nom.
. **mumtāzatun** (ممتازةٌ) *excellent:* adjective, agrees with **fikratun** (فكرةٌ) → fem. sing. nom. indef.

***This** [is] the picture of the new house.*
hād͟hihi ṣūrat-u -l-bayt-i -l-jadīd-i (هذه صورة البيت الجديد).
. **hād͟hihi** (هذه) *this [near the speaker]:* demonstrative pronoun, agrees with antecedent **ṣūratu** (صورةُ) → fem. sing. def., subj. in verbless sentence → nom.
. **ṣūratu** (صورةُ) *picture:* noun, fem. sing., 1st term of gen. construct → def., predicate in verbless sentence → nom.
. **-l-bayti** (البيتِ) *(of) the house:* noun, masc. sing. def., 2nd term of gen. construct → gen.
. **-l-jadīd-i** (الجديدِ) *new:* adjective, agrees with **-l-bayti** (البيتِ) → masc. sing. gen. def.

*I bought some apples; I'm giving you **these two**.*
'i-s͟htaray-tu baᶜḍ-a -l-tuffāḥ-i; sa-'uᶜṭī-ka **hāt-ayni**.
(اشتريت بعض التفاح؛ سأعطيك هاتين)
. **'i-s͟htaraytu** (اشتريتُ) *I bought:* verb, 1st pers. sing., perfect
. **baᶜḍa** (بعض) *some:* noun, masc., sing., obj. of **'i-s͟htaraytu** (اشتريتُ) → acc.
. **-l-tuffāḥi** (التفاح) *apples:* collective noun → masc. sing. def., 2nd term of gen. construct → gen.
. **sa** (س)- *will:* future particle
. **'uᶜṭī** (أعطي) *I give:* verb, 1st pers. sing., imperfect
. **-ka** (كَ) *you:* suffixed pronoun, 2nd pers. sing., ind. obj. of **'uᶜṭī** (أعطي) → acc.
. **hātayni** (هاتين) *these two [near the speaker]:* demonstrative pronoun, agrees with implied antecedent **tuffāḥatayni** (تفاحتين) *two apples* → fem. dual, obj. of **'uᶜṭī** (أعطي) ,→ acc.

*Who [is] **that man**?*
man **dhālika -l-rajul-u** (من ذلكَ الرجلُ)?
- **man** (من) *who?:* interrogative pronoun, subj. in verbless sentence
- **dhālika** (ذلكَ) *that [away from speaker and addressee]:* demonstrative pronoun, agrees with antecedent **-l-rajulu** (الرجلُ) → masc. sing. nom.
- **-l-rajulu** (الرجلُ) *man:* noun, masc. sing., predicate in verbless sentence → nom.

*I came with **those students**.*
ji'-tu ma^ca **'ulā'ika -l-ṭullāb-i**. (جئت مع ألائك الطلاب)
- **ji'tu** (جئت) *I came:* verb, 1st pers. sing., perfect
- **ma^ca** (مع) *with:* preposition
- **'ula'ika** (ألائك) *those [away from speaker and addressee]:* demonstrative pronoun, agrees with antecedent **-l-ṭullābi** (الطلابِ)→ masc. pl. gen.
- **-l-ṭullābi** (الطلابِ) *students:* noun, masc. pl. def., obj. of **ma^ca** (مع)→ gen.

CHAPTER

24

WHAT IS A RELATIVE PRONOUN?

A **RELATIVE PRONOUN** is a word used at the beginning of a clause that gives additional information about someone or something previously mentioned.

clause:
additional information about *the book*

I'm reading the book *that* the teacher recommended.

IN ENGLISH

A relative pronoun serves two purposes:

1. As a pronoun it stands for a noun previously mentioned. The noun to which it refers is called the **ANTECEDENT.**

 This is the boy *who* broke the window.

 antecedent of the relative pronoun *who*

2. It introduces a **SUBORDINATE CLAUSE** — that is, a group of words having a subject and a verb that cannot stand alone because it forms part of a **MAIN CLAUSE** — that is, another group of words having a subject and a verb which can stand alone as a complete sentence.

 main clause — subordinate clause

 Here comes the boy *who broke the window.*

 verb antecedent subject verb

A subordinate clause which starts with a relative pronoun is called a **RELATIVE CLAUSE.** In the example above, the relative clause starts with the relative pronoun *who* and gives us additional information about the antecedent *boy.*

A different relative pronoun is used when the antecedent is a person or a thing.

PERSON — The form of some relative pronouns changes depending on the pronoun's function in the relative clause.

- subject of the relative clause → *who* or *that*

 This is the hero *who* won the war.

 antecedent subject of *won*

- object in the relative clause → *whom* or *that* (in parentheses because as an object it is often omitted in English)

  This is the pirate *[whom]* Sinbad killed.

  antecedent object of *killed*

- possessive form → *whose*

  This is the woman *whose* novel we read.

  antecedent possessive modifying *novel*

THING — The form of the relative pronoun doesn't change → *which* or *that*

- subject of the relative clause → always expressed

  This is the book *which* is so interesting.

  antecedent subject of *is*

- object in the relative clause → in parentheses because it is often omitted

  This is the book *[that]* I bought.

  antecedent object of *bought*

COMBINING SENTENCES WITH RELATIVE PRONOUNS

A relative pronoun allows us to combine two clauses that have a common element into a single sentence. Notice that the antecedent always stands immediately before the relative pronoun that introduces the relative clause. The relative pronoun functions as subject or object or possessive in the relative clause.

- subject of relative clause

  SENTENCE A That is the *hero.*
  SENTENCE B *He* won the war.

You can combine Sentences A and B by replacing the subject pronoun *he* with the relative pronoun *who.*

  That is the hero *who won* the war.

  antecedent relative clause

- object in relative clause

  SENTENCE A That is the *pirate.*
  SENTENCE B Sinbad killed *him.*

You can combine Sentences A and B by replacing the object pronoun *him* with the relative pronoun *whom.* We have placed *whom* and *that* between parentheses because relative pronoun objects are often omitted in English.

That is the pirate *[whom]* Sinbad killed.
That is the pirate *[that]* Sinbad killed.

antecedent — relative clause

- object of preposition

SENTENCE A This is *the teacher.*
SENTENCE B I studied Arabic with *her.*

You can combine sentences A and B by replacing *her* with *whom* and placing *with whom* after the antecedent.

That is the teacher *with whom* I studied Arabic.

antecedent — relative clause

- relative pronoun as possessive

SENTENCE A This is *the student.*
SENTENCE B I borrowed *his* books.

You can combine sentences A and B by replacing *his* with *whose* and placing *whose books* after the antecedent.

That is the student *whose books* I borrowed.

antecedent — relative clause

IN ARABIC

Unlike English, the same forms of the relative pronoun serve for both persons and things: the definite article **'a-l-** (ال) + a form of the pronoun **la<u>dh</u>ī** (الذي) .

Unlike English that often omits a relative pronoun functioning as an object, Arabic always expresses a relative pronoun, regardless of its function, providing its antecedent is definite. When the antecedent is indefinite no relative pronoun is used.

Here are two examples in which we inserted the English relative pronoun between brackets because it is optional in English; it is required, however, in an Arabic sentence with a definite antecedent.

This [is] ***the book*** *[that] you want.*

definite antecedent → a form of **'a-l-la<u>dh</u>ī** (الذي)

This [is] ***a book*** *[that] you want.*

indefinite antecedent → no Arabic relative pronoun

In addition, there is an important difference in structure between English and Arabic. Arabic requires a separate reference to the antecedent in the relative clause, thus turning the English subordinate clause into an independent clause. As a result, the relative pronoun is no longer part of either clause, but merely serves as a link between two independent clauses (see p. 146 in *What are Phrases, Clauses and Sentences?*).

Here are examples of ways to refer to the antecedent in Arabic relative clauses.

- by inserting in the relative clause a pronoun object of the verb referring to the antecedent

  independent clause — dependent clause
  This is the teacher ***[that]*** *I had last term.*
  ARABIC →
  independent clause — independent clause
  This is the teacher that I had ***her*** *last term.*
  antecedent — pronoun referring to *teacher*

- by inserting a pronoun object of a preposition referring to the antecedent in the relative clause

  independent clause — dependent clause
  This is the teacher ***[that]*** *we studied Arabic with.*
  ARABIC →
  independent clause — independent clause
  This is the teacher that we studied Arabic with ***her****.*
  antecedent — pronoun referring to *teacher*

- by using a verb form that agrees with the antecedent

  independent clause — dependent clause
  Don't buy the ticket ***[that]*** *costs too much.*
  ARABIC →
  independent clause — independent clause
  Don't buy the ticket that ***it*** *costs too much.*
  antecedent — verb 3rd pers. sing. agreeing with *ticket*

In Arabic the relative pronoun agrees with its antecedent in gender, number and definiteness and takes its case from its own function in the clause. Below are the steps to follow to chose the appropriate Arabic relative pronoun.

I know the book ***[that]*** *you want.*

1. Find the antecedent: *book*
2. Antecedent gender + number: **'a-l-kitāb-u** (الكتابُ) *the book* → masc. sing.
3. Antecedent definite or indefinite: *the book*
   a. definite → go to step 4.
   b. indefinite → go to step 5.

4. Select form of relative pronoun: masc. sing. → **'al-ladhī** (الذي)
5. Create two independent clauses:
   a. 1st clause: *I know* ***the book***
   b. 2nd clause with reference to antecedent: *book* → *you want* ***it***
6. Combine 1st clause (5a) + relative pronoun (4) + 2nd clause (5b)

'aʿrif-u –l-kitāb-a **–l-ladhī** turīd-u-hu (أعرف الكتاب الذي تريده) .

- **'aʿrifu** (أعرف) *I know*: verb, 1st per. sing., imperfect
- **-l-kitāba** (الكتابَ) *the book*: noun, masc. sing. def., obj. of **aʿrifu** (أعرف) → acc.
- **-l-ladhī** (الذي) *that*: relative pronoun, masc. sing.
- **turīdu** (تريد) *you want:* verb, 2nd pers. masc. sing., imperfect
- **-hu** (هُ) *it*: suffixed pronoun, 3rd pers. masc. sing., obj. of **turīdu** (تريد) → acc.

Here are some examples. You can use the chart below as reference.

GENDER: NUMBER:	Masc.	Fem.
Singular	'al-ladhī (الذي)	'al-latī (التي)
Dual		
Nom.	'al-ladhāni (اللذان)	'al-latāni (اللتان)
Gen./Acc.	'al-ladhayni (اللذَين)	'al-latayni (اللتَين)
Plural	'al-ladhīna (الذين)	'al-lātī (التي), 'al-lawā tī (اللواتي)

- subject of relative clause with definite antecedent

Where are the [male] athletes ***who came from Sudan?***

1. Antecedent: *athletes*
2. Gender + number: **lāʿibūna** (لاعبونَ) *athletes* → masc. pl.
3. Definite or indefinite: *the athletes* → def.
4. Form of relative pronoun: masc. pl. → **'al-ladhīna** (الذينَ)
5. Two independent clauses:
   1st clause: *where are* ***the athletes***
   2nd clause with reference to antecedent: *athletes* → ***they*** *came from Sudan*
6. Combine 1st clause + relative pronoun + 2nd clause

'ayna –l-lāʿib-ūna **–l-ladhīna** jā'-ū min -l-sūdān-i?
(اين اللاعبون الذين جاؤا من السودان؟)

- **'ayna** (أين) *where?*: adverb
- **–l-lāʿibūna** (اللاعبونَ) *the athletes*: noun, masc. pl. def., subj. → nom.
- **–l-ladhīna** (الذين) *who*: relative pronoun, masc. pl.
- **jā'ū** (جاؤا) *(they) came*: verb, 3rd pers. masc. pl., perfect
- **min** (من) *from*: preposition
- **-l-sūdāni** (السودان) *Sudan*: proper noun, masc. sing. def., obj. of **min** (من) → gen.

- subject of relative clause with indefinite antecedent

These [are] women athletes ***who came from Tunisia.***

1. Antecedent: *athletes*

2. Gender + number: **lāᶜibātun** (لاعباتٌ) *athletes* → fem. pl.
3. Definite/indefinite: *athletes* → indef.
4. Form of relative pronoun: indef. go to step 5
5. Two independent clauses:
   1st clause: *these are* ***women athletes***
   2nd clause with reference to antecedent: *athletes* → ***they*** *came from Tunisia*
6. Combine 1st clause + 2nd clause

hā'ulā'i lāᶜibāt-u-n **ḥaḍar-na** min tūnis-a (هؤلاء لاعباتٌ حضرنَ من تونسَ)

- **hā'ulā'i** (هؤلاء) *these [near the speaker or the addressee]*: demonstrative pronoun, pl.
- **lāᶜibātun** (لاعباتٌ) : *athletes*: noun, fem. pl. indef., predicate → nom.
- **ḥaḍarna** (حضرنَ) *(they) came*: verb, 3rd pers. fem. pl., perfect
- **min** (من) *from*: preposition
- **tūnisa** (تونسَ) *Tunisia*: proper noun, obj. of **min** (من) → gen.

■ direct object in relative clause

The athletes ***[that]*** *you saw in Morocco arrived yesterday.*

1. Antecedent: *athletes*
2. Gender + number: **lāᶜibūna** (لاعبونَ) *athletes* → masc. pl.
3. Definite/indefinite: *the athletes* → def.
4. Form of relative pronoun: masc. pl. → **'al-la<u>dh</u>īna** (الذينَ)
5. Two independent clauses:
   1st clause: ***the athletes*** *arrived yesterday*
   2nd clause with reference to antecedent: *athletes* → *you saw* ***them*** *in Morocco*

6 Combine 1st clause + relative pronoun + 2nd clause

waṣal-a 'amsi –l-lāᶜib-ū-na **l-a<u>dh</u>īna** <u>sh</u>āhad-ta-**hum** fī -l-ma<u>gh</u>rib-i (وصل امس اللاعبون الذين شاهدتهم في المغرب).

- **waṣala** (وصل) *(he) arrived:* verb, 3rd pers. masc., verb precedes subj. → sing., perfect
- **'amsi** (امس) *yesterday:* adverb
- **-l-lāᶜibūna** (اللاعبونَ) *the athletes:* noun, masc. pl. def., subj. of **waṣala** (وصل) → nom.
- **-l-la<u>dh</u>īna** (الذينَ) *who*: relative pronoun, masc. pl.
- **<u>sh</u>āhadta** (شاهدت) *you saw:* verb, 2nd pers. masc. sing., perfect
- **-hum** (هم) *them:* suffixed pronoun, 3rd pers. masc. pl., dir. obj. of **<u>sh</u>āhadta** (شاهدت) → acc.
- **fī** (في) *in:* preposition
- **-l-ma<u>gh</u>ribi** (المغرب) *Morocco:* noun, masc. sing. def., obj. of **fī** (في)→ gen.

■ indirect object in relative clause

Who [are] the athletes ***[that]*** *they will award the prize to?*

1. Antecedent: *athletes*
2. Gender + number: **lāᶜibūna** (لاعبونَ) *athletes* → masc. pl.
3. Definite/indefinite: *the athletes* → def.
4. Form of relative pronoun: masc. pl. → **'al-la<u>dh</u>īna** (الذينَ)

5. Two independent clauses:
   1st clause: *who are* ***the athletes***
   2nd clause with reference to antecedent: *athletes* → *they will award* ***them*** *the prize*
6. Combine 1st clause + relative pronoun + 2nd clause

man -l-lāᶜibūna **-l-ladhīna** sa-yamnaḥ-ūna-**hum** -l-jā'izat-a?
(من اللاعبون الذين سيمنحونهم الجائزة؟)

- **man** (من) *who?:* interrogative pronoun, subj. in verbless sentence
- **-l-lāᶜibūna** (اللاعبونَ) *the athletes:* noun, masc. pl. def., predicate → nom.
- **–l-ladhīna** (الذينَ) *who*: relative pronoun, masc. pl., agrees with antecedent **-l-lāᶜibūna** (اللاعبونَ) → masc. pl.
- **sa** (س)- *will:* future particle
- **yamnaḥūna** (يمنحونَ) *they award:* verb, 3rd pers. masc. pl., imperfect
- **-hum** (هم) *them:* suffixed pronoun, ind. obj. of **yamnaḥūna** (يمنحونَ) → acc.
- **-l-jā'izata** (الجائزة) *the prize:* noun, fem. sing. def., dir. obj. of **yamnaḥūna** (يمنحونَ) → acc.

■ object of preposition in relative clause

Where [are] the [male] athletes ***[that]*** *Walid trained with?*

1. Antecedent: *athletes*
2. Gender + number: **lāᶜibūna** (لاعبونَ) *athletes* → masc. pl.
3. Definite/indefinite: *the athletes* → def.
4. Form of relative pronoun: masc. pl. → **'al-ladhīna** (الذينَ)
5. Two independent clauses:
   1st clause: *where are* ***the athletes***
   2nd clause with reference to antecedent: *athletes* → *Walid trained with* ***them***
6. Combine 1st clause + relative pronoun + 2nd clause

'ayna–l-lāᶜibūna **-l-ladhīna** tadarrab-a maᶜa-**hum** walīd-u-n?
(اين اللاعبون الذين تدرب معهم وليد؟)

- **'ayna** (أين) *where?*: interrogative adverb
- **-l-lāᶜibūna** (اللاعبونَ) *the athletes*: noun, masc. pl. def., subj. in verbless sentence → nom.
- **-l-ladhīna** (الذينَ) *who*: relative pronoun, agrees with antecedent **-l-lāᶜibūna** (اللاعبونَ) → masc. pl.
- **tadarraba** (تدربَ) *(he) trained*: verb, 3rd pers. mas. sing., perfect
- **maᶜa** (معَ) *with*: preposition
- **-hum** (هم) *them*: suffixed pronoun, masc. pl., obj. of **maᶜa** (معَ)→ gen.
- **walīdun** (وليدٌ) *Walid*: proper noun, masc. sing. def., subj. of **tadarraba** (تدربَ) → nom.

CHAPTER

25

WHAT IS A VERB?

A **VERB** is a word that indicates the action of the sentence. The word "action" is used in its broadest sense, not necessarily physical action.

Let us look at different types of meanings of verbs:

• a physical activity	to run, to hit, to talk, to walk
• a mental activity	to hope, to believe, to imagine, to dream, to think
• a condition	to be, to feel, to have, to seem

Many verbs, however, do not fall neatly into one of the above three categories. They are verbs nevertheless because they represent the "action" of the sentence.

The book *costs* only $5.00.
to cost

It is important to identify verbs because the function of words in a sentence often depends on their relationship to the verb. For instance, the subject of a sentence is the word doing the action of the verb and the object is the word receiving the action of the verb (see *What is a Subject?*, p. 32 and *What are Objects?*, p. 36).

IN ENGLISH

The verb is the most important word in the sentence. You cannot compose a **COMPLETE SENTENCE** without a verb. To help you learn to recognize verbs, look at the paragraph below where verbs are in *italics.*

The three students *entered* the restaurant, *selected* a table, *hung* up their coats and *sat* down. They *looked* at the menu and *asked* the waiter what he *recommended.* He *suggested* the daily special, the falafel plate. It *was* not expensive. They *ordered* hummus and, for a salad, tabbouleh. The service *was* slow, but the food *tasted* very good. Good cooking, they *decided, takes* time. They *had* baklava for dessert and *finished* the meal with Arabic coffee. They *felt* happy!

IN ARABIC

Verbs are identified the same way as they are in English and, like English, most Arabic sentences require a verb. However, an Arabic verb has many more forms than an English verb (see *What is a Verb Conjugation?*, p. 90) and, unlike English, Arabic has sentences without verbs (see *What is a Predicate Word?*, p. 34).

FORM SYSTEM – The Form System permits the extension of the meaning of the basic root of a verb. For example, by inserting the basic root **K-T-B** into a different pattern, namely 'aCCaC, **katab-a** (كتب) *he wrote (to write)* can be expanded to **'aktab-a** (اكتب) *he dictated something to someone.*

Arabic verbs are classified into ten different patterns, each one called a **FORM** ("F" in "Form" to differentiate it from the term "verb form"). Form I, or the Basic Form, contains only the three consonants of the root plus a vowel or two. Each of the nine derived patterns, called **DERIVED FORMS** and numbered Form II to X, creates a different meaning related to the meaning of the basic verb.

No basic verb has derived verbs in every Form because some Forms are not compatible with the meaning of the root. Your textbook will provide the various meanings of each Form.

Here is an example of the perfect tense of the various derived Forms of the Arabic verb root **K-T-B** (كتب) *write.* Notice that the change of Form is reflected in the stem of the verb (in **bold**), but that the inflections remain the same. Since a word pronounced in isolation or at the beginning of a sentence cannot start with two consonants, the stems of Forms VII, VIII and X, that start with two consonants, are preceded by a glottal stop (') + the "helping vowel" **i**-. The hyphen following the "**i**" indicates that it is a **HELPING VOWEL** meaning that the vowel is dropped when it follows another word.

FORM I: **katab**-ū (كَتَبوا) *they wrote*
[activity of the root]

FORM II: **kattab**-ū (كَتّبوا) *they made (s.o.) write*
[cause s.o. to do the root activity]

FORM III: **kātab** -ū (كاتبوا) *they corresponded with (s.o)*
[involve s.o. in the root activity]

FORM IV: **'aktab**-ū (أكتبوا) *they dictated (something to s.o.)* [cause s.o. to do the root activity]

FORM VI: **takātab-ū** (تكاتبوا) *they corresponded with each other* [reciprocal action of root activity]

FORM VII: **'i-nkatab-ū** (انْكتبوا) *they subscribed to* [to cause oneself to do the root activity]

FORM VIII: **'i-ktatab-ū** (اكْتتبوا) *they copied s.th. down* [to do the root activity for oneself]

FORM X: **'i-staktab-ū** (اسْتكتبوا) *they asked s.o. to write s.th.* [to ask s.o. to do the root activity]

As you can see above, Forms V and IX are missing because those derived Forms are not compatible with the meaning of the basic verb.

CAREFUL — In English it is possible to change the meaning of a verb by placing short words (prepositions or adverbs) after it. For example, the verb *look* in Column A below changes meaning depending on the word that follows it *(at, for, after, into)*. A different Arabic verb corresponds to each meaning.

COLUMN A	MEANING	ARABIC
to look *at* →	to view I *looked at* the photo.	**na<u>dh</u>ara 'ilā** (نظر إلى)
to look *for* →	to search for I *am looking for* a book.	**baḥa<u>th</u>-a ʿan** (بحث عن)
to look *after* →	to take care of I *am looking after* the children.	**'iʿtanā bi-** (اعتنى بِ)
to look *into* →	to study We*'ll look into* the problem.	**baḥa<u>th</u>-a fī** (بحث في)

When consulting an English-Arabic dictionary, all the examples under Column A can be found under the dictionary entry *look*; you will have to search under that entry for the specific expression *look for* or *look after,* etc. to find the correct Arabic equivalent. Don't select the first entry under *look* and then add on the Arabic equivalent for *after, for, into,* etc.; the result will be meaningless in Arabic.

TERMS USED TO TALK ABOUT VERBS

- **DICTIONARY FORM** — In English, the form of the verb listed in the dictionary is the name of the verb: *eat, sleep, drink* (see *What are Infinitives and Gerunds?,* p. 93). In Arabic, the form of the verb listed in the dictionary is the 3rd person masculine singular of the perfect tense, equivalent to: *he ate, he slept, he drank* (see p. 89 in *What are the Principal Parts of a Verb?*). In this handbook we use the Arabic dictionary form, followed by the literal translation and the English infinitive in parentheses: **katab-a** (كتبَ) *he wrote (to write).*

- **CONJUGATION** — A verb is conjugated or changes in form to agree with its subject: *I do, he does* (see *What is a Verb Conjugation?*, p. 90).
- **FORM** — In English, a verb is identified by its person, number and tense. In Arabic, a verb is also identified by its gender.
- **PERSON** — A verb form is identified by the "person," a human being or a thing that is doing the action of the verb (see p. 57 in *What is a Subject Pronoun?*). .
- **NUMBER** — A verb form indicates the number of "persons" doing the action of the verb (*What is Meant by Number?*, p. 16).
- **GENDER** — In Arabic, a verb form indicates the gender of the "person(s)" doing the action of the verb (see *What is Meant by Gender?*, p. 13).
- **INFLECTION** — In Arabic, verbs are inflected; that is, by adding prefixes and suffixes the verb indicates, among other things, the doer of the action (see *What is a Verb Conjugation?*, p. 90).
- **TENSE** — A verb indicates tense; that is, the time the action of the verb takes place (present, past, or future): *I am, I was, I will be* (see *What is Meant by Tense?*, p. 103).
- **MOOD** — A verb shows mood; that is, the speaker's attitude toward what he or she is saying (see *What is Meant by Mood?*, p. 126).
- **VOICE** — A verb shows voice; that is, the relation between the subject and the action of the verb (see *What is Meant by Active and Passive Voice?*, p. 123).
- **TRANSITIVITY** — A verb is classified as transitive (abb. *tr.)* if it can take a direct object and intransitive (abb. *int.)* if it cannot cannot take a direct object (see *What are Objects?*, p. 36).

CHAPTER

26

WHAT ARE THE PRINCIPAL PARTS OF A VERB?

The **PRINCIPAL PARTS** of a verb are the forms we need in order to create all the different tenses (see *What is Meant by Tense?*, p. 103).

IN ENGLISH

English verbs have three principal parts:

1. the dictionary form (the infinitive without "to")
2. the past tense
3. the past participle

If you know these parts, you can form all the other tenses of that verb (see *What are Infinitives and Gerunds?*, p. 93; *What is the Past Tense?*, p. 109, and pp. 95-6 in *What is a Participle?*).

English verbs fall into two categories depending on how they form their principal parts:

REGULAR VERBS — These verbs are called regular because the forms of their past tense and past participle follow the predictable pattern of adding *-ed*, *-d*, or *-t* to the infinitive.

DICTIONARY	PAST TENSE	PAST PARTICIPLE
walk	walk*ed*	walk*ed*
bake	bake*d*	bake*d*
burn	burn*ed* (burn*t*)	burn*ed* (burn*t*)

Since the past tense and the past participle are identical, regular verbs have only two principal parts: the infinitive and the past.

IRREGULAR VERBS — These verbs are called irregular because their principal parts do not follow a regular pattern.

DICTIONARY	PAST TENSE	PAST PARTICIPLE
be	was	been
sing	sang	sung
go	went	gone
write	wrote	written

IN ARABIC

Unlike English, all Arabic verbs are regular, that is, there is only one conjugation pattern for all verbs in the language. (Roots that have "w" or "y" as one of their radicals undergo changes in pronunciation that follow regualar rules, as will be illustrated in your textbook.) All verbs have three principal parts.

For example:

kataba (u) (katbun, kitbatun, kitābatun) *to write*
(كتبَ) | (كتْبٌ) (كتبةٌ) (كتابةٌ)
1 2 3

1. **Dictionary form** — The first principal part is the 3rd person masculine singular of the perfect tense verb, for example **kataba** (كتبَ) *he wrote*. This part gives you the stem, **katab-**(كتب), to which you will add the perfect tense endings. It is the form under which a verb is listed in dictionaries and glossaries because it is the shortest form of a verb. In the dictionary, verbs are entered in alphabetical order according to the first letter of the root (see p. 7).
2. **Stem vowel of the imperfect tense** — The second principal part is the imperfect tense stem vowel, i.e., the vowel that comes immediately before the last consonant of the stem (see *What is the Present Tense?*, p. 106). For example, the imperfect stem of **kataba** (كتبَ) *he wrote* is **-ktvb-** *write*, where "v" stands for the stem vowel to be replaced by **-u-**, giving you the imperfect stem **-ktub-** (كتُب) *write*. This is the stem to which you will add the imperfect tense endings: **'a-ktub-u** (أكْتُبُ) *I write*, etc. (see *What is a Verb Conjugation?*, p. 90).
3. **Verbal nouns** — The third principal part listed between parentheses gives you the forms of the verb when it functions as a noun (see *What are Infinitives and Gerunds?*, p. 93). Each verbal noun has a different pattern and, therefore, slightly different meanings. For example: **katbun** (كتْبٌ) *writing* (noun masc. sing.), **kitbatun** (كتبةٌ) *way of writing* (noun fem. sing.) and **kitābatun** (كتابةٌ) *customary activity of writing* (noun fem. sing.).

It is important to memorize the principal parts of a verb in order to be able to conjugate it in the different tenses.

CHAPTER 27

WHAT IS A VERB CONJUGATION?

A **VERB CONJUGATION** is a list of the six possible forms of the verb for a particular tense. For each tense, there is one verb form for each of the pronouns used as the subject of the verb.

I am
you are
he, she, it is
we are
you are
they are

Different tenses have different verb forms, but the principle of conjugation remains the same. In this chapter all our examples are in the present tense (see *What is the Present Tense?*, p. 106).

IN ENGLISH

The verb *to be* is the English verb which changes the most; it has three forms: *am, are,* and *is*. The initial vowel is often replaced by an apostrophe: *I'm, you're, he's*. Other English verbs only have two forms, the verb *to sing* for instance.

SINGULAR		
	1ST PERSON	I *sing*
	2ND PERSON	you *sing*
	3RD PERSON	he *sings* she *sings* it *sings*
PLURAL		
	1ST PERSON	we *sing*
	2ND PERSON	you *sing*
	3RD PERSON	they *sing*

Because English verbs change so little, it isn't necessary to learn "to conjugate a verb" — that is, to list all its possible forms. For most verbs, it is much simpler to say that the verb adds an "-s" in the 3rd person singular.

IN ARABIC

Unlike English, Arabic verbs add different prefixes and suffixes to identify the person of the verb (see p. 57), the gender and the number of the subject (see pp. 58-60) and the mood of the verb (see p. 126). These prefixes and suffixes are called **INFLECTIONS.**

A conjugated verb consists of the following parts:

1. STEM — The stem of the verb identifies the dictionary meaning of the verb and the tense (see p. 7).
2. SUFFIXES — The suffixes indicate the person, number and/or gender of the subject, and for the imperfect tense the mood of the verb.
3. PREFIXES — The prefixes of the imperfect tense, one of the two Arabic tenses, indicate the person and in some cases the number and/or gender of the subject (see *What is the Present Tense?*, p. 106). The other tense, the perfect, does not have prefixes (see *What is the Past Tense?*, p. 109).

Here is an example of the conjugation of a basic Form in the imperfect tense (the Arabic imperfect tense corresponds to English present tense, see p. 106). Notice that prefixes and suffixes are separated from the stem by hyphens.

FORM I: **katab-a** (كتب) *he wrote (to write)*
IMPERFECT STEM: **-ktub-** (كتب)

		Prefix	Stem	Gndr + No.	Mood (Indic.)		
SINGULAR							
1ST PERSON		'a-	-ktub-	–	-u	(أكتبُ)	*I write*
2ND PERSON	(masc.)	ta-	-ktub-	–	-u	(تكتبُ)	*you write*
	(fem.)	ta-	-ktub-	-ī	-na	(تكتبين)	*you write*
3RD PERSON	(masc.)	ya-	-ktub-	–	-u	(يكتبُ)	*he writes*
	(fem.)	ta-	-ktub-	–	-u	(تكتبُ)	*she writes*
DUAL							
2ND PERSON		ta-	-ktub-	-ā	-ni	(تكتبانِ)	*you write*
3RD PERSON	(masc.)	ya-	-ktub-	-ā	-ni	(يكتبانِ)	*they write*
	(fem.)	ta-	-ktub-	-ā	-ni	(تكتبانِ)	*they write*
PLURAL							
1ST PERSON		na-	-ktub-	–	-u	(نَكتبُ)	*we write*
2ND PERSON	(masc.)	ta-	-ktub-	-ū	-na	(تكتبون)	*you write*
	(fem.)	ta-	-ktub-	-na	–	(تكتبْنَ)	*you write*
3RD PERSON	(masc.)	ya-	-ktub-	-ū	-na	(يكتبون)	*they write*
	(fem.)	ya-	-ktub-	-na	–	(يكتبن)	*they write*

Notice that each of the thirteen forms has its own set of inflections, except for **ta-ktub-u** (تكتبُ) 2nd pers. masc. sing., *you write,* and 3rd pers. fem. sing., *she writes,* which must be distinguished by the context.

All Arabic verbs, regardless of their Form, use the same inflections to indicate the person, gender and number of their subject and the mood of the verb. As another example, here is the conjugation in the imperfect tense of a derived Form (see p. 85) of **katab-a** (كتبَ) *he wrote (to write).*

FORM VIII: **'i-ktatab-a** (اكْتَتِبَ) *he copied (to copy)*
IMPERFECT STEM: **-ktatib-** (كْتَتِب)

		Prefix	Stem	Gndr + No.	Mood (Indic.)		
SINGULAR							
1ST PERSON		'a-	-ktatib-	–	-u	(اكْتَتِبُ)	*I copy*
2ND PERSON	**(masc.)**	ta-	-ktatib-	–	-u	(تكتتب)	*you copy*
	(fem.)	ta-	-ktatib-	-ī	-na	(تكتتبين)	*you copy*
3RD PERSON	**(masc.)**	ya-	-ktatib-	–	-u	(يكتتبُ)	*he copies*
	(fem.)	ta-	-ktatib-	–	-u	(تكتتبُ)	*she copies*
DUAL							
2ND PERSON		ta-	-ktatib-	-ā	-ni	(تكتتبانِ)	*you copy*
3RD PERSON	**(masc.)**	ya-	-ktatib-	-ā	-ni	(تكتتبونَ)	*they copy*
	(fem.)	ta-	-ktatib-	-ā	-ni	(تكتتبْنَ)	*they copy*
PLURAL							
1ST PERSON		na-	-ktatib-	–	-u	(نَكْتُبُ)	*we copy*
2ND PERSON	**(masc.)**	ta-	-ktatib-	-ū	-na	(تكتتبونَ)	*you copy*
	(fem.)	ta-	-ktatib-	-na	–	(تكتتبْنَ)	*you copy*
3RD PERSON	**(masc.)**	ya-	-ktatib-	-ū	-na	(يكتتبونَ)	*they copy*
	(fem.)	ya-	-ktatib-	-na	–	(يكتتبنَ)	*they copy*

CHAPTER 28

WHAT ARE INFINITIVES AND GERUNDS?

The **INFINITIVE** is a form of the verb without person or tense, expressing the verb's basic meaning: *to study, to read, to write.* A **GERUND** is another form that is part verb and part noun: *studying, reading, writing.*

IN ENGLISH

INFINITIVE — The infinitive, without the preceding "to," is the **DICTIONARY FORM**, i.e., the form under which a verb is listed in the dictionary: *love, walk, take.* The infinitive, usually preceded by "to," is used as a noun, that is as the subject or object of a conjugated verb (see *What is a Verb Conjugation?*, p. 90).

To learn *is* exciting.

infinitive subject of verb *is* — conjugated verb

Fawzi and Shireen *want* to dance together.

conjugated verb — infinitive object of verb *want*

After verbs such as *must, let* or *can* "to" is omitted.

Fawzi must *be* home by noon.

dictionary form

I might *be* late tomorrow.

dictionary form

The mother lets her children *watch* television.

dictionary form

GERUND — The gerund is a verbal noun; that is, a noun derived from a verb by adding *-ing* to the dictionary form of the verb: *learning, dancing, talking.* Like the infinitive it can serve as subject or object; unlike the infinitive, however, some gerunds can be made plural.

Dancing is good exercise.

gerund → subject of *is*

I like *going* to football games.

gerund → object of *like*

His *goings* and *comings* irritated us.

plural gerunds → subjects of *irritated*

IN ARABIC

Like the English infinitive and gerund, Arabic verbal nouns (sometimes called **maṣdar** (مصدر)) are derived from verbs and function as both nouns and verbs. The verbal noun takes the case appropriate to its function in the sentence, but its own subject and object are put in the genitive case (see genitive construct, pp. 23, 30). Here are a few examples.

***Dancing** [is] good exercise.*
'al-raqṣ-u tamrīn-u-n nāfiᶜu-n (الرقْص تمرينٌ نافعٌ).

- **'al-raqṣu** (الرقْص) *dancing:* verbal noun, masc. sing. def., subj. in verbless sentence → nom.
- **tamrīnun** (تمرينٌ) *exercise:* verbal noun, masc. sing., predicate → nom. indef.
- **nāfiᶜun** (نافعٌ) *useful:* adjective, agrees with **tamrīnun** (تمرينٌ) → masc. sing. nom. indef.

*Mohammad's **departure** astonished us.*
'adhash-at-nā **mughādarat-u** muḥammad-i-n (أدْهشتنا مُغادَرةُ مُحَمَّدٍ).

- **'adhashat** (أدْهشت) *(she) astonished:* verb, 3rd fem. sing., perfect
- **-nā** (نا) *us:* suffixed pronoun, 1st pers. pl., obj. of **'adhashat** (أدْهشت) → acc.
- **mughādaratu** (مُغادَرةُ) *departure:* verbal noun, fem. sing., 1st term of gen. construct → def., subj. of **'adhashat** (أدْهشت)→ nom.
- **muḥammadin** (مُحَمَّدٍ) *Muhammad's:* proper noun, masc. sing. def., subj. of **mughādaratu** (مُغادَرةُ)→ gen.

*She finished **writing** the report yesterday.*
'akmal-at 'amsi **kitābat-a** -l-taqrīr-i (أكْملتْ أمْس كتابةَ التقريرِ) .

- **'akmalat** (أكْملتْ) *she finished:* verb, 3rd pers. fem. sing., perfect
- **'amsi** (أمْس) *yesterday:* adverb
- **kitābata** (كتابةَ) *(the) writing:* verbal noun, fem. sing., 1st term in gen. construct → def., obj. of **'akmalat** (أكْملتْ) → acc.
- **-l-taqrīri** (التقريرِ) *(of) the report:* noun, masc. sing. def., 2nd term in gen. construct → gen.

*They thanked us for **going** to the airport.*
shakar-ū-nā ᶜalā **dhahāb-i-nā** 'ilā -l-maṭār-i.(شَكرونا على ذهابِنا الى المطارِ)

- **shakarū** (شَكرو) *they thanked:* verb, 3rd pers. masc. pl., perfect
- **-nā** (نا) *us:* suffixed pronoun, 1st pers. pl., obj. of **shakarū** (شَكرو)→ acc.
- **ᶜalā** (على) *for:* preposition
- **dhahābi** (ذهابِ) *going:* verbal noun, masc. sing. def., 1st term in gen. construct → def., obj. of **ᶜalā** (على) → gen.
- **-nā** (نا) suffixed pronoun, 1st pers. pl., subj. of verbal noun → gen.
- **'ilā** (إلى) *to:* preposition
- **-l-maṭāri** (المطارِ) *the airport:* noun, masc. sing. def., obj. of **'ilā** (إلى) → gen.

Your textbook will introduce you to the many different verbal noun patterns and their usages.

CHAPTER 29

WHAT IS A PARTICIPLE?

A **PARTICIPLE** is a form of a verb that can be used in one of two ways: with an auxiliary verb to form certain tenses or as an adjective to describe something.

He *has closed* the door.

auxiliary + participle → present perfect tense

He heard me through the *closed* door.

participle describing *door* → adjective

Since participles function as both adjectives and verbs they are also called **VERBAL ADJECTIVES**.

IN ENGLISH

In English, there are two types of participles: the present participle and the past participle.

PRESENT PARTICIPLE — The present participle is easy to recognize because it is the *-ing* form of the verb: work*ing*, study*ing*, danc*ing*, play*ing*.

The present participle has two primary uses:

1. as the main verb in compound tenses with forms of the auxiliary *to be* to indicate the progressive tenses (see *What is an Auxiliary Verb?*, p. 99 and *What are the Progressive Tenses?*, p. 121).

   She *is writing* a report.

   present progressive of *to write*

   They *were studying*.

   past progressive of *to study*

2. as an adjective describing a noun or pronoun (see *What is an Adjective?*, p. 40)

   Farid is a *singing* waiter.

   describes the noun *waiter*

   He woke the *sleeping* child.

   describes the noun *child*

PAST PARTICIPLE — The past participle is formed in several ways. It is the form of the verb that follows *has* or *have*: he has *spoken*, I have *walked*, we have *written*.

The past participle has two primary uses:

1. as the main verb in compound tenses with forms of the the auxiliary verb *to have* to indicate perfect tenses: the present perfect tense (see p. 117), the past perfect tense (see p. 118) and the future perfect tense (see p. 119)

   I *have written* all that I have to say.
   present perfect of *to write*

   He *hadn't spoken* to me since our quarrel.
   past perfect of *to speak*

2. as an adjective describing a noun or pronoun

   Is that a *corrected* text?
   describes the noun *text*

   Is the *written* or *spoken* word more important?
   describe the noun *word*

IN ARABIC

Arabic has two participles: an active participle and a passive participle (see *What Is Meant by Active and Passive Voice?*, p. 123). Since participles are adjectives, they can modify nouns and pronouns, and, like all Arabic adjectives, they agree with them in gender, number, case and definiteness.

ACTIVE PARTICIPLE — Let us look at an example of how to form the active participle of a Form I verb (see *What is a Verb?*, p. 84). The root is inserted in the pattern **CāCiC**.

> VERB: **darasa** (دَرَسَ) *he studied (to study)*
> ROOT + PATTERN: D-R-S + CāCiC → **DāRiS-**(دارس)
> ACTIVE PARTICIPLE: **dāris-un** (دارسٌ) *having studied*
>
> VERB: **shaghala** (شغَلَ) *he occupied (to occupy)*
> ROOT + PATTERN: SH-GH-L + CāCiC → **SHāGHiL-**(شاغل)
> ACTIVE PARTICIPLE: **shāghil-un** (شاغلٌ) *occupying*

An active participle is used when the modified noun performs the action of the verb. For example, in *the man wearing a cloak*, the man is wearing the cloak, i.e., he is performing the action of "wearing a cloak."

Here is an example.

> *They [are] the students **coming** from Algeria.*
> hum -l-ṭullāb-u **-l-qādim-ūna** min -l-jazā'ir-i.
> (هم الطلّابُ القادمون من الجَزائرِ)

- **hum** (هم) *they:* independent pronoun, 3rd pers. masc pl., subj. in verbless sentence → nom.
- **l-ṭullābu** (الطلّابُ) *the students:* noun, masc. pl. def., predicate → nom.
- **-l-qādimūna** (القادمون) *coming:* active participle, agrees with **-l-ṭullābu** (الطلّابُ) → masc pl. def. nom.
- **min** (من) *from*: preposition
- **-l-jazā'iri** (الجَزائرِ) *Algeria:* proper noun, fem. sing. def., obj. of **min** (من) → gen.

Unlike English, where active participles as main verbs are only used in progressive tenses, the active participle of Arabic verbs can have a variety of possible meanings; for instance, some active participles can express a completed action, a future progressive or future action, etc. (see also p. 119 in *What are the Perfect Tenses?* and *What are the Progressive Tenses?*, p. 121). As you come across these meanings for a particular active participle, make a note of them.

Passive participle — Let us look at an example of how to form the passive participle of a Form I verb. The root is inserted in the pattern **maCCūC**.

Verb: **darasa** (دَرَسَ) *he studied (to study)*
Root + pattern: D-R-S + maCCūC → **maDRūS-** (مدْروس)
Passive participle: **madrūs-u-n** (مدْروسٌ) *(having been) studied*

Verb: **shaghala** (شغل) *he occupied (to occupy)*
Root + pattern: SH-GH-L + maCCūC → **maSHGHūL-**(مشْغول)
Passive participle: **mashghūl-u-n** (مشْغولٌ) *occupied, busy*

A passive participle is used when the modified noun receives the action of the verb. For example, in *a cloak worn by the man,* the cloak is being worn, i.e., it is the receiver of the action of "wearing."

Here is an example.

What [is] the meaning of the sentence ***written*** *on the blackboard?*
mā maʿnā -l-jumlat-i **-l-maktūbat-i** ʿalā -l-lawḥ-i?
(ما معْنى الجُمْلة المكتوبةِ على اللوْحِ؟)

- **mā** (ما) *what?:* interrogative pronoun subject
- **maʿnā** (معْنى) *the meaning*: noun, masc. sing., 1st term in gen. construct → def., predicate in verbless sentence→ nom.
- **-l-jumlati** (الجُمْلة) *of the sentence*: noun, fem. sing. def., 2nd term in gen. construct → gen.
- **-l-maktūbati** (المكتوبةِ) *written*: passive participle, agrees with **-l-jumlati** (الجُمْلة) → fem. sing. def. gen.
- **ʿalā** (على) *on:* preposition
- **-l-lawḥi** (اللوْحِ) *the blackboard:* noun, masc. sing. def., obj. of **ʿalā** (على)→ gen.

Your textbook will show you how to create active and passive participles from derived Form verbs.

CAREFUL — Never assume that an English word ending in *-ing* will be translated by an Arabic active participle; it might be an imperfect tense verb, a verbal noun or a common noun.

- word with *-ing* used with a form of *to be* with progressive meaning → active participle in Arabic or an imperfect tense (see *What are the Progressive Tenses?*, p. 121)

  He ***is meeting*** *with the doctor.*

  present progressive

  mujtami^c-u-n (مجتمعٌ)

  active participle of Form VIII (see p. 86 in *What is a Verb Conjugation?*)

  Who ***is using*** *the cell phone?*

  present progressive

  yasta^cmil-u (يستعمل)

  imperfect of **'i-sta^cmal-a** (استعمل) *he used (to use)*

- word with *-ing* used as an attributive adjective → active participle in Arabic

  The teacher ***meeting*** *with the parent is Mr. Simsim.*

  attributive adjective

  'a-l-mujtami^c-u (المجتمع)

  active participle of Form VIII

- word with *-ing* used as a subject or object of verb or preposition → verbal noun in Arabic

  Meeting *the musicians was a unique experience.*

  subject of verb *was*, dir. obj. *the musicians*

  'a-l-ijtimā^cu bi- (الاجتماع بِ)

  verbal noun

- word with *-ing* used as a common noun that can be made plural → verbal noun in Arabic

  The meetings *were many and long but fruitless.*

  common noun pl.

  'a-l-ijtimā^cāt-u (الاجتماعات)

  verbal noun pl.

CHAPTER 30

WHAT IS AN AUXILIARY VERB?

A verb is called an **AUXILIARY VERB** or **HELPING VERB** when it helps another verb, called the **MAIN VERB**, form one of its tenses.

He *has been gone* two weeks.
(*has been* = auxiliary verbs; *gone* = main verb)

A verb tense composed of an auxiliary verb plus a main verb is called a **COMPOUND TENSE**.

IN ENGLISH

There are three verbs which can be used as auxiliaries: *to have, to be* and *to do*. Auxiliary verbs serve different purposes:

1. *to have* — to create different perfect tenses (see *What are the Perfect Tenses?*, p. 117)
   - present of *to have* → present perfect

     I ***have*** *read* the book.
   - past of *to have* → past perfect

     I ***had*** *read* the book before I left.
   - future of *to have* → future perfect

     I ***will have*** *read* the book by the end of the week.
2. *to be* — to create different progressive tenses and to form the passive voice (see *What are the Progressive Tenses?*, p. 121; *What is Meant by Active and Passive Voice?*, p. 123)
   - present of *to be* + present participle → present progressive

     Zaynab ***is*** *reading* about Arab history.
   - past of *to be* + present participle → past progressive

     Zaynab ***was*** *reading* about Arab history.
   - present, past, future of *to be* + past participle → passive voice

     Arabic ***is*** *spoken* here.
     Arabic ***was*** *spoken* here.
     Arabic ***will be*** *spoken* here.

3. *to do* — to create the emphatic forms of the present and past tenses (see *What is the Present Tense?*, p. 106 *What is the Past Tense?*, p. 109)

    Zaynab ***does** like* to speak Arabic.
    Zaynab ***did** like* to speak Arabic as a child.

- *to do* — to formulate questions and negative sentences (see *What are Affirmative, Negative, Declarative and Interrogative Sentences?*, p. 153)

    Does Zaynab *read* books?
    Zaynab ***does** not read* books.

IN ARABIC

Arabic has only one auxiliary verb, **kān-a** (كان) *he was* (*to be*). As in English, **kān-a** (كان) serves to change the tense of the main verb.

PAST IMPERFECT — the perfect tense of **kān-a** (كان) + imperfect tense of main verb (see pp. 110-1 in *What is the Past Tense?*)

***He used to speak** well.*
past tense
kān-a yatakallam-u jayyid-a-n (كان يتكلم جيداً).
. **kāna** (كان) *he was:* auxiliary verb, 3rd pers. masc. sing., perfect
. **yatakallamu** (يتكلمُ) *(he) speaks*: main verb, 3rd pers. masc. sing., imperfect

***She was writing** a letter.*
past progressive
kān-at taktub-u risālat-a-n (كانت تكتبُ رسالةً).
. **kānat** (كانت) *she was:* auxiliary verb, 3rd pers. fem. sing., perfect
. **taktubu** (تكتبُ) *(she) writes:* main verb, 3rd pers. fem. sing., imperfect

PAST PERFECT — the perfect tense of **kān-a** (كان) + **qad** (قد) + perfect tense of main verb (see What are the Perfect Tenses?, pp. 118-9)

***They had spoken** before class.*
kān-ū qad takallam-ū qabl-a -l-ṣaff-i (كانوا قد تكلموا قبل الصفّ).
. **kānū** (كانوا) *they were:* auxiliary verb, 3rd pers. masc. pl., perfect
. **qad** (قد): perfective particle
. **takallamū** (تكلموا) *they spoke:* main verb, 3rd pers. masc. pl., perfect

FUTURE PERFECT — the future tense of **kān-a** (كان) + **qad** (قد) + perfect tense of main verb (*see What are the Perfect Tenses?*, pp. 119-20)

*They **will have spoken** before class.*
sa-yakūn-ūna qad takallam-ū qabl-a -l-ṣaff-i.
(سيكونون قد تكلموا قبل الصف)
. **sa-** (س) *will:* future particle
. **yakūnūna** (يكونون) *they will be:* auxiliary verb, 3rd pers. masc. pl., imperfect
. **qad** (قد): perfective particle
. **takallamū** (تكلموا) *(they) spoke:* main verb, 3rd pers. masc. pl., perfect

MODALS

Arabic and English also have a series of auxiliary verbs called MODALS, such as *will, would, may, might, can, could, must,* that are used to modify the meaning of the main verb.

IN ENGLISH

Modals modify the meaning of the main verb by indicating modes such as possibility, probability, necessity, etc. They are followed by the infinitive (without "to") of the main verb.

Can you *help* me with this sentence?
He *might forget* the appointment without a reminder.
They *should join* us for dinner today.
You *must finish* this paper before the end of the term.

IN ARABIC

As in English, Arabic modals modify the meaning of the main verb. However, instead of indicating the possibility or necessity of doing the action of the main verb, Arabic modals generally relate to the beginning of the action of the verb. The modals are either in the perfect or the imperfect tense and are always followed by the main verb in the imperfect, both agreeing with the subject. The tense of the modal sets the time of the main verb, i.e., a modal in the imperfect sets the time in the present and a modal in the perfect sets the time in the past.

- *to begin* — **bada'-a** (بدأ) or **'akhadh-a** (أخذ) or **'aṣbaḥ-a** (أصبح)+ imperfect of main verb

*The students **began studying** the day before the exam.*
bada'-a -l-ṭullāb-u **yadrus-ūna** -l-yawm-a qabl-a -l-i-mtiḥān-i. (بدأ الطلاب يدرسون اليوم قبل الامتحان)
. **bada'a** (بدأ) *(he) began:* modal verb, 3rd pers. masc., verb precedes subj. → sing., perfect
. **-l-ṭullābu** (الطلاب) *the students:* noun, masc. pl. def., subj. of **bada'a** (بدأ)→ nom.

- **yadrusūna** (يدرسون) *they study:* main verb, 3rd pers. masc. pl., imperfect
- **-l-yawma** (اليوم) *the day:* noun, masc. sing. def., expression of time → acc.
- **qabla** (قبل) *before:* preposition
- **-l-i-mtiḥāni** (الامتحان) *the exam:* verbal noun, masc. sing. def., obj. of **qabla** (قبل) → gen.

■ *almost* — **'awshak-a 'an** (أوشك أن) or **kād-a** (كاد) + imperfect of main verb

*She **almost died** from laughing.*
kād-at tamūt-u min -l-ḍaḥik-i (كادت تموت من الضحك).

- **kā dat** (كادت) *she was about to:* modal verb, 3rd pers. fem. sing., perfect
- **tamūtu** (تموت) *she dies:* main verb, 3rd pers. fem. sing., imperfect
- **min** (من) *from:* preposition
- **-l-ḍaḥiki** (الضحك) *laughing:* verbal noun, masc. sing. def., obj. of **min** (من) → gen.

*She **almost falls.***
tūshik-u 'an taqa^c-a (توشك أن تقع).

- **tūshiku** (توشك) *she is about to:* modal verb, 3rd pers. fem. sing., imperfect
- **'an** (أن) *that:* conjunction + subjunctive
- **taqa^ca** (تقع) *she fall:* verb, 3rd pers. fem. sing., subjunctive

CAREFUL — The English auxiliaries *to have* and *to do* do not exist as auxiliaries in Arabic. See the various sections referred to above for equivalent Arabic structures and tenses.

CHAPTER

31

WHAT IS MEANT BY TENSE?

The **TENSE** of a verb indicates when the action of the verb takes place: at the present time, in the past, or in the future.

I am studying	PRESENT
I studied	PAST
I will study	FUTURE

As you can see in the above examples, just by putting the verb in a different tense and without giving any additional information (*I am studying* = now, *I studied* = before, *I will study* = later), you can indicate when the action of the verb takes place.

Tenses may be classified according to the way they are formed. A **SIMPLE TENSE** consists of only one verb form (I *studied),* while a **COMPOUND TENSE** consists of one or more auxiliaries plus the main verb (I *am studying,* I *had been studying*).

In this section we will only consider tenses of the indicative mood (see *What is Meant by Mood?,* p. 126).

IN ENGLISH

Listed below are the main tenses of the indicative mood whose equivalents you will encounter in Arabic:

PRESENT TENSES	
I study	PRESENT
I do study	PRESENT EMPHATIC
I am studying	PRESENT PROGRESSIVE
PAST TENSES	
I studied	SIMPLE PAST
I did study	PAST EMPHATIC
I was studying	PAST PROGRESSIVE
FUTURE TENSE	
I will study	FUTURE
PERFECT TENSES	
I have studied	PRESENT PERFECT
I had studied	PAST PERFECT
I will have studied	FUTURE PERFECT

As you can see, there are only two simple tenses, i.e., the present and the simple past. All of the other tenses are compound tenses.

IN ARABIC

Listed below are the Arabic tenses that you will encounter.

		ARABIC TENSE:
PRESENT		
'adrus-u (أدرسُ)	*I study, I do study* *I am studying*	IMPERFECT
PAST		
daras-tu (درستُ)	*I studied, I did study*	PERFECT
kun-tu 'adrus-u (كنتُ أدرسُ)	*I studied, I used to study, I was studying*	PAST IMPERFECT
FUTURE		
sa-'adru-su (سأدرسُ)	*I will study*	FUTURE
PERFECT TENSES		
qad daras-tu (قد درستوا)	*I have studied*	PRESENT PERFECT
kun-tu qad daras-tu (كنت قد درستوا)	*I had studied*	PAST PERFECT
sa-'akūn-u qad darast-u (سأكون قد درستوا)	*I will have studied*	FUTURE PERFECT

As you can see, Arabic has only two simple tenses; i.e., the imperfect and the perfect. All the other Arabic tenses are compound tenses based on these two tenses: they are formed with the Arabic auxiliary **kān-a** (كان) *he was (to be)* + the main verb in the imperfect tense or with **qad** (قد), known as "the perfective particle," + the main verb in the perfect tense (see *What is an Auxiliary Verb?*, p. 99).

As reference, here is a list of English tenses, their equivalent Arabic tense or tenses and the chapter in which they are discussed.

ENGLISH — present → ARABIC — imperfect (see *What is the Present Tense?*, p. 106)

I write, am writing, do write

present → imperfect

'aktub-u (أكتبُ)

ENGLISH — past → ARABIC — perfect or past imperfect (see *What is the Past Tense?*, p. 109)

***I wrote** her last week.*

one time in the past → perfect

katab-tu ... (كتبتُ)

***I wrote** her every week.*

habitual action in the past → past imperfect

kun-tu 'aktub-u ... (كنت أكتب)

. **kuntu** (كنت) *I was:* auxiliary verb, 1st pers. sing., perfect

. **'aktubu** (أكتبُ) *I write:* main verb, 1st pers. sing., imperfect

ENGLISH — future → ARABIC — future (see *What is the Future Tense?*, p. 113)

> ***I will/shall/am going to/write*** *you soon.*
> **sa-'aktub-u ...** (سأكتبُ)
> . **sa-** (س) *will:* future particle
> . **'aktubu** (أكتبُ) *I write:* verb, 1st pers. sing., imperfect

ENGLISH — present perfect → ARABIC — present perfect (see *What are the Perfect Tenses?*, p. 117)

> ***I have written*** *five letters so far.*
> **qad katab-tu ...** (قد كتبتُ)
> . **qad:** (قد)perfective particle
> . **katabtu** (كتبتُ) *I wrote:* verb, 1st pers. sing., perfect

ENGLISH — past perfect → ARABIC — past perfect (see *What are the Perfect Tenses?*, p. 117)

> ***I had written*** *that two years earlier.*
> **kun-tu qad katab-tu ...** (كنت قد كتبت)
> . **kuntu** (كنت) *I was:* auxiliary verb, 1st pers. sing., perfect
> . **qad**: (قد)perfective particle
> . **katabtu** (كتبتُ)*I wrote:* main verb, 1st pers. sing., perfect

ENGLISH — future perfect → ARABIC — future perfect (see *What are the Perfect Tenses?*, p. 117)

> ***I will have written*** *the letter before you come.*
> **sa-'akūn-u qad katab-tu ...** (سأكون قد كتبت)
> . **sa -** (س) *will:* future particle
> . **'akūnu** (أكون) *I will be:* auxiliary verb, 1st pers. sing., imperfect
> . **qad**: (قد)perfective particle
> . **katabtu** (كتبتُ) *I wrote:* main verb, 1st pers. sing., perfect

CHAPTER 32

WHAT IS THE PRESENT TENSE?

The **PRESENT TENSE** indicates that the action is happening at the present time. It can be at the moment the speaker is speaking, a habitual action, a state or condition, or a general truth.

PRESENT TIME	I *see* you.
HABITUAL ACTION	He *smokes* constantly.
CONDITION OR STATE	He *seems* tired.
GENERAL TRUTH	The sun *rises* every day.

IN ENGLISH

There are three forms of the verb that are present tense. Each form has a different meaning:

SIMPLE PRESENT	Huda *studies* in the library.
PRESENT PROGRESSIVE	Huda *is studying* in the library.
PRESENT EMPHATIC	Huda *does study* in the library.

Depending on the information requested in a question, you will automatically choose one of the three forms above in your answer.

Where does Huda study? She *studies* in the library.
Where is Huda now? She *is studying* in the library.
Does Huda study in the library? Yes, she *does* [*study* in the library].

IN ARABIC (see *What are the Principal Parts of a Verb?*, p. 88 and *What is a Verb Conjugation?*, p. 90)

In Arabic the equivalent of the English present tense is the imperfect tense. Arabic verbs in the imperfect are inflected for person, number and gender of the subject and for mood (for person see p. 57, for number and gender see conjugation below, and for mood see p. 126). The set of imperfect tense inflections is the same for all basic and derived Forms (see Forms, p. 85).

For example, all Form I verbs have the imperfect stem pattern **CCvC**, where the C's represent the three consonants of the root and "v" repesents a short stem vowel. Here is an example of how to form the imperfect stem of a basic Form, followed by the conjugation of the imperfect.

DICTIONARY ENTRY: **daras-a** (**u**) (دَرَسَ) *he studied (to study)*
ROOT: **D-R-S**

INSERT ROOT IN IMPERFECT TENSE PATTERN: C → **D**, C → **R**, v, C → **S** → **-drvs-**
REPLACE "v": **-u-** (between parentheses in dictionary entry)
IMPERFECT STEM: **-drus-**(درُس)

		Prefix	Stem	Gender + No.	Mood (Indic.)		
SINGULAR							
1ST PERSON		'a-	-drus-	–	-u	(أَدْرُسُ)	*I study*
2ND PERSON	(masc.)	ta-	-drus-	–	-u	(تَدْرُسُ)	*you study*
	(fem.)	ta-	-drus-	-ī	-na	(تَدْرسينَ)	*you study*
3RD PERSON	(masc.)	ya	-drus-	–	-u	(يدرسُ)	*he studies*
	(fem.)	ta-	-drus-	–	-u	(تدرسُ)	*she studies*
DUAL							
2ND PERSON		ta-	-drus-	-ā	-ni	(تدرسانِ)	*you study*
3RD PERSON	(masc.)	ya-	-drus-	-ā	-ni	(يدرسانِ)	*they study*
	(fem.)	ta-	-drus-	-ā	-ni	(تدرسانِ)	*they study*
PLURAL							
1ST PERSON		na-	-drus-	–	-u	(ندرسُ)	*we study*
2ND PERSON	(masc.)	ta-	-drus-	-ū	-na	(تدرسونَ)	*you study*
	(fem.)	ta-	-drus-	-na	–	(تدرسنَ)	*you study*
3RD PERSON	(masc.)	ya-	-drus-	-ū	-na	(يدرسونَ)	*they study*
	(fem.)	ya-	-drus-	-na	–	(يدرسْنَ)	*they study*

See p. 91 for another example of the conjugation of a basic Form in the imperfect tense.

The English present tenses have the following Arabic equivalents.

*We always **study** in the library.*

present [habitual action]
nadrus-u (ندرسُ)
imperfect of **daras-a** (درَس) *he studied (to study)*

*Who **is using** the cell phone?*

present progressive
yastaʿmil-u (يستعمل)
imperfect of **'i-staʿmal-a** (استعمل) *he used (to use)*

***I do like** bananas!*

present emphatic
'uḥibb-u (احبُّ)
imperfect of **'aḥabb-a** (احبَّ) *he loved (to love)*

CAREFUL — Do not assume that the English equivalents of all Arabic verbs in the imperfect tense are in the present tense. The English equivalent depends on whether the Arabic verb in the imperfect tense is in a main or in a subordinate clause. If it is in a main clause it is an English present tense. However, if it is in a subordinate clause the English equivalent could be a past tense (see *What is a Conjunction?*, p. 140 and p. 146 in *What are Phrases, Clauses and Sentences?*).

main clause

Mariam ***is studying*** *at the library.*

present progressive

maryam-u **tadrus-u** fī -l-maktabat-i . (مريم تدرسُ في المكتبة)

main verb imperfect → present time

main clause — subordinate clause

He said *that Mariam* ***was studying*** *in the library.*

past — past progressive

qāl-a (قالَ) — **tadrus-u** (تدرسُ)

he said — *is studying*

main verb: perfect — subordinate clause: imperfect → past time

CHAPTER
33

WHAT IS THE PAST TENSE?

The **PAST TENSE** is used to express an action that occurred prior to the moment of speaking.

> I *saw* you yesterday.

IN ENGLISH

There are several tenses that indicate that the action took place in the past.

I worked	SIMPLE PAST
I did work	PAST EMPHATIC
I was working	PAST PROGRESSIVE

The simple past is a simple tense; that is, it consists of one word (ex. *worked*). It has two meanings:

> I *took* a bus yesterday.
>
> single completed action in the past
>
> I always *took* the bus to work.
>
> habitual (repeated) action in the past

The other past tenses are compound tenses; that is, they consist of more than one word (ex. *was working, did work, had worked*).

IN ARABIC

In Arabic, the perfect and the past imperfect tenses indicate that an action took place prior to the moment of speaking.

PERFECT TENSE — The perfect is a simple tense. Like all Arabic verbs, it is inflected for person, number and gender (see *What is a Verb Conjugation?*, p. 90). The set of perfect tense inflections is the same for all basic and derived Forms (see Forms, p. 85).

Let's look at an example. Notice that the perfect tense, unlike the imperfect tense, has no prefixes.

> VERB: **daras-a** (دَرَسَ) *he studied (to study)*
> STEM OF PERFECT: **daras-** (درس)

		Stem	Person/Gender/Number		
SINGULAR					
1ST PERSON		daras-	tu	(دَرَسْتُ)	*I studied*
2ND PERSON	(masc.)	daras-	ta	(درستَ)	*you studied*
	(fem.)	daras-	ti	(درستِ)	*you studied*
3RD PERSON	(masc.)	daras-	a	(دَرَسَ)	*he studied*
	(fem.)	daras-	at	(دَرَسَتْ)	*she studied*
DUAL					
2ND PERSON		daras-	tumā	(درستما)	*you studied*
3RD PERSON	(masc.)	daras-	ā	(درسا)	*they studied*
	(fem.)	daras-	atā	(درستا)	*they studied*
PLURAL					
1ST PERSON		daras-	nā	(درسنا)	*we studied*
2ND PERSON	(masc.)	daras-	tum	(درستم)	*you studied*
	(fem.)	daras-	tunna	(درستنّ)	*you studied*
3RD PERSON	(masc.)	daras-	ū	(درسوا)	*they studied*
	(fem.)	daras-	na	(درسْنَ)	*they studied*

The perfect tense denotes a completed act or event; it answers the question "What happened?" Here are some examples.

> ***I studied** yesterday with Rami.*
>
> 1st pers. sing. perfect → **daras-tu** (دَرَسْتُ)
>
> *Mariam **graduated** from the American University.*
>
> 3rd pers. fem. sing. perfect→ **takharraj-at** (تخرجت)
>
> ***We recognized** the new visitor.*
>
> 1st pers. pl. perfect → **ʿaraf-nā** (عرفنا)

The English past emphatic is expressed in Arabic by adding the emphatic particle **la-** (ل) to the perfective particle **qad** (قد) + the perfect tense.

> ***I did work** as a teacher.*
> **la-qad ʿamiltu** (لقد عملتُ)

PAST IMPERFECT — The past imperfect is a compound tense formed with the auxiliary verb **kān-a** (كان) *he was (to be)* in the perfect tense + the main verb in the imperfect tense. Both the auxiliary verb and the main verb agree with the subject; for example: (1st pers. pl. perfect) **kun-nā** (كنا) + (1st pers. pl. imperfect) **na-ktub-u** (نكتُبُ) *we wrote, used to write, were writing.*

> AUXILIARY VERB: **kān-a** (كان) *he was (to be)*
> STEM OF PERFECT: **kān-**(كان) (before a vowel), **kun-**(كن) (before a consonant)

		Perfect kāna (كان)		Imperfect darasa (دَرَسَ)		
SINGULAR						
1ST PERSON		kun-tu	(كُنْتُ)	'adrus-u	(أدْرُسُ)	*I used to study*
2ND PERSON	(masc.)	kun-ta	(كنتَ)	tadrus-u	(تَدْرُسُ)	*you used to study*
	(fem.)	kun-ti	(كنتِ)	tadrus-īna	(تَدْرُسِينَ)	*you used to study*
3RD PERSON	(masc.)	kān-a	(كان)	yadrus-u	(يدرسُ)	*he used to study*
	(fem.)	kān-at	(كانت)	tadrus-u	(تدرسُ)	*she used to study*
DUAL						
2ND PERSON		kun-tumā	(كنتما)	tadrus-āni	(تدرسانِ)	*you used to study*
3RD PERSON	(masc.)	kān-ā	(كانا)	yadrus-āni	(يدرسانِ)	*they used to study*
	(fem.)	kān-atā	(كانتا)	tadrus-āni	(تدرسانِ)	*they used to study*
PLURAL						
1ST PERSON		kun-nā	(كنّا)	nadrus-u	(ندرسُ)	*we used to study*
2ND PERSON	(masc.)	kun-tum	(كنتُم)	tadrus-ūna	(تدرسونَ)	*you used to study*
	(fem.)	kun-tunna	(كنتنّ)	tadrus-na	(تدرسْنَ)	*you used to study*
3RD PERSON	(masc.)	kān-ū	(كانوا)	yadrus-ūna	(يدرسونَ)	*they used to study*
	(fem.)	kun-na	(كنّ)	yadrus-na	(يدرسْنَ)	*they used to study*

The past imperfect tense may denote a past habitual action, a past progressive, or a past condition. It answers the question "How were things?"
Here are some examples.

__I used to study__ with Rami.

habitual action in the past
1st pers. sing. → **kun-tu 'adrus-u** (كنت ادرسُ)

Mariam __was studying__ in the library.

past progressive
3rd pers. fem. sing. → **kān-at tadrus-u** (كانت تدرسُ)

***I knew** all the names.*

past condition
1st pers. sing. → **kun-tu 'aʿrif-u** (كنت اعرفُ)

PERFECT VS. PAST PERFECT

The Arabic equivalent of an English verb in the past tense can be either in the perfect or the past imperfect. Which of these two tenses is appropriate in Arabic depends on how the verb is used in the particular English sentence.

The perfect is used when the purpose of the verb is to state that an event took place, i.e., to tell what happened, often using expressions related to the specific time the action took place, such as *this morning, last month, when I got to class,* etc.

The past imperfect is used when the purpose of the verb is to describe how things used to be or what was going on, often using expressions related to frequency of the action, such as *always, usually, often, never, every day,* etc.

For example, the Arabic equivalent of *I knew* could be ᶜ**araf-tu** (عرفتُ) (perfect → an event) or **kun-tu 'a**ᶜ**rifu** (كنت اعرفُ)(past imperfect→past state). Here are a few guidelines to select the correct tense.

- If the English past tense cannot be replaced with *used to* or *would* + the dictionary form of the verb without changing the meaning of the verb → perfect tense.

  I ***knew*** *him the moment he entered the room.*

  It answers the question: What happened? You can't substitute *I knew* with *I used to know. "I used to know him* the moment he entered the room." *I knew* → perfect → ᶜ**araftu** (عرفتُ)

- If the English past tense can be replaced with *used to* or *would* + the dictionary form of the verb without changing the meaning of the verb → past imperfect tense.

  I ***knew*** *him like a brother.*

  It answers the question: How were things? You can substitute *I knew* with *I used to know. "I used to know him like a brother." I knew* → past imperfect → **kuntu 'a**ᶜ**rif-u** (كنت اعرفُ)

- If the English verb is in the past emphatic form (ex. *did work)* → perfect tense.

  I did see him.

  ra'ay-tu (رأيتُ)

- If the English verb is a past progressive tense (ex. *was working)* → past imperfect.

  What ***were you doing?***

  2nd pers. masc. sing. → **kun-ta taf**ᶜ**al-u** (كنت تفعلُ)

- In a sentence when one action is interrupted by another: the action that was going on → past imperfect tense; the action that is interrupting → perfect tense.

  I was studying *when* ***I fell asleep.***

kun-tu 'adrus-u (كنت أدرسُ)	**ghafī-tu** (غفيتُ)
What was going on? → past imperfect	What happened? → perfect

Consult your Arabic textbook for additional guidelines on the forms and usage of the past tenses.

CHAPTER

34

WHAT IS THE FUTURE TENSE?

The **FUTURE TENSE** predicts that an action will take place some time in the future.

> I*'ll see* you tomorrow.

IN ENGLISH

The future tense is formed with the auxiliary *will* or *shall* + the dictionary form of the main verb. Note that *shall* is used in formal English (and British English), and *will* in everyday language. In conversation, *shall* and *will* are often shortened to *'ll.*

> Gibran *will do* his homework tomorrow.
> I*'ll leave* tonight.

A future action can also be expressed with *to go* in present progressive tense + the dictionary form of the main verb (see *What are the Progressive Tenses?*, p. 121).

> Gibran *is going to do* his homework tomorrow.
> I*'m going to leave* tonight.

Occasionally, the present tense is used to refer to an action which may take place in the future.

> She *leaves* for Morocco next week.

IN ARABIC

The future tense is a simple tense formed with the future prefix **sa-** (سَ) or **sawfa** (سوف) + the imperfect of the main verb (see *What is the Present Tense?*, p. 106). It corresponds to the English future tense as well as to the *going to* construction.

> *The instructor* ***will explain*** *everything.*
> *The instructor* ***is going to explain*** *everything.*

sa-yufassir-u (سيفسرُ)

future of **fassar-a** (فسّر) *he explained (to explain)*

Verbs of motion *(to go, to travel)* can also use the active participle to express the future (see *What is a Participle?*, p. 95).

> ***I'll travel*** *to Algeria next year.*
> ***I'm going to travel*** *to Algeria next year.*

I'm traveling *to Algeria next year.*
sa-'usāfir-u ... (سأسافرُ)

future of **sāfar-a** (سافَرَ) *he traveled (to travel)*
'anā musāfir-u-n (أنا مسافرٌ)

active participle of **sāfar-a** (سافَرَ)

FUTURE OF PROBABILITY

IN ENGLISH

The idea of probability is expressed with words such as *must, probably, I wonder.*

My keys *must be* around here.
My keys *are probably* around here.

IN ARABIC

In Arabic the future tense is used to express what the speaker feels is probably true. This use of the future is called the **FUTURE OF PROBABILITY**. For present time, the future of probability is formed with the future tense of **kān-a** (كان) *he was (to be):* **sa-yakūn-u** (سيكون) *he will be.* For a completed action, the future of probability is formed with the future perfect tense (see p. 119 in *What are the Perfect Tenses?*).

I wonder *where my book* ***is.***

present time

'ayna **sa-yakūn-u** kitāb-ī (اين سيكون كتابي؟)?

- **'ayna** (أين) *where?:* interrogative adverb
- **sa-** (س) *will:* future prefix
- **yakūnu** (يكون) *(he) will be:* verb, 3rd pers. masc. sing., imperfect
- **kitāb(-u)** (كتاب) *book:* noun, masc. sing. def., subj. of **sa-yakūnu** (سيكون) → nom. [**kitābu** (كتابُ) + **-ī** (ي) → **kitābī** (كتابي)]
- **- ī** (ي) *my:* suffixed pronoun, possessive, 2nd term in gen. construct → gen.

Karima ***must have taken*** *it.*

completed action

sa-takūn-u karīmat-u **qad 'a<u>kh</u>a<u>dh</u>-at**-hu (ستكون كريمة قد اخذته)

- **sa-** (س) *will:* future prefix
- **takūnu** (تكون) *(she) will be:* auxiliary verb, 3rd pers. fem. sing., imperfect
- **karīmatu** (كريمةُ) *Karima:* proper noun, fem. sing. def., subj. of **sa-takūnu qad 'a<u>kh</u>a<u>dh</u>athu** (ستكون قد اخذته) → nom.
- **qad** (قد) : perfective particle
- **'a<u>kh</u>a<u>dh</u>at** (اخذت) *(she) took:* main verb, 3rd pers. fem. sing., perfect
- **-hu** (هُ) *it:* suffixed pronoun, 3rd pers. masc. sing., obj. of **sa-takūnu qad 'a<u>kh</u>a<u>dh</u>at** (ستكون قد اخذت) → acc.

FUTURE-IN-THE-PAST

IN ENGLISH

When the point of reference is in the past—an action to take place after another action in the past—it is called the FUTURE-IN-THE-PAST. This is expressed by *would* + the dictionary form of the main verb or *was going to* + the dictionary form of the main verb.

In both sentences below, Mustafa is going to go to Mecca at some future point. In the first sentence, the future is relative to the present ("Mustafa *says*..."); in the second sentence, the future time is relative to the past ("Mustafa *said*...").

Mustafa *says* he *will go* to Mecca.
Mustafa *says* he *is going to go* to Mecca.

present — future

Mustafa *said* he *would go* to Mecca.
Mustafa *said* he *was going to go* to Mecca

past — future-in-the-past

IN ARABIC

In Arabic, verbs can express the future-in-the-past with the auxiliary verb **kān-a** (كان) *he was (to be)* in the perfect tense + the future of the main verb. Both the auxiliary verb and the main verb agree with the subject; for example: (1st pers. pl. perfect) **kun-nā** (كنا) + (1st pers. pl. future) **sa-naktub-u** (سنكتبُ) *we were going to write.*

The instructor ***was going to explain*** *everything.*
kān-a l-mudarris-u **sa-yufassir-u** kull-a shay'-i-n.
(كان المدرس سيفسر كل شيءٍ)

- **kāna** (كان) *(he) was:* auxiliary verb, 3rd pers. masc. sing., perfect
- **l-mudarrisu** (المدرس) *the instructor:* noun, masc. sing. def., subj. of **sa-yufassiru** (سيفسر)→ nom.
- **sa** (س)- *will:* future prefix
- **yufassiru** (يفسر) *(he) explains:* main verb, 3rd pers. masc. sing., imperfect
- **kulla** (كل) *every:* noun, masc. sing. def., obj. of **yufassiru** (يفسر) → acc.
- **shay'in** (شيءٍ) *thing:* noun, masc. sing. indef., 2nd term of gen. construct → gen.

Verbs of motion *(to go, to travel)* can also use the active participle to express the future-in-the-past.

I said *[that]* ***I was going to go*** *to Algeria next year.*
qul-tu 'inna-nī **sa-'adhhab-u** 'ilā -l-jazā'ir-i -l-sanat-a -l-qādimat-a. (قلت انني سأذهب الى الجزائر السنة القادمة)

- **qultu** (قلتُ) *I said:* main verb, 1st pers. sing., perfect

- **'inna** (ان) *that:* subordinating conjunction + acc. subj.
- **-nī** (ني) *I:* suffixed pronoun, 1st pers. sing., subj. of **'inna** (ان) → acc.
- **sa** (س)-: future prefix
- **'adhhabu** (أذهب) *I go*: verb, 1st pers. sing, imperfect
- **'ilā** (إلى) *to:* preposition
- **-l-jazā'iri** (الجزائر) *Algeria*: proper noun, fem. sing. def., obj. of **'ilā** (إلى) → gen.
- **-l-sanata** (السنة) *the year*: noun, fem. sing. def., noun used as time expression → acc.
- **-l-qādimatā** (القادمة) *the coming*: adjective, agrees with **-l-sanata** (السنة) → fem. sing. def. acc.

***I said** [that]**I would go** to Algeria next year.*
qul-tu 'inna-nī **dhāhib-u-n** 'ilā -l-jazā'ir-i -l-sanat-a -l-qādimat-a. (قلت انني ذاهب الى الجزائر السنة القادمة)

- **qultu** (قلتُ) *I said:* main verb, 1st pers. sing., perfect
- **'inna** (ان) *that:* subordinating conjunction + acc. subj.
- **-nī** (ني) *I:* suffixed pronoun, 1st pers. sing., subj. of **'inna** (ان) → acc.
- **dhāhibun** (ذاهبٌ) *going*: active participle, masc. sing., predicate in verbless sentence → nom. indef.
- (see above)

CHAPTER 35

WHAT ARE THE PERFECT TENSES?

The **PERFECT** tenses are compound tenses formed with the auxiliary *have* indicating that the action of the verb is completed.

I *have eaten* today.
present perfect

I *had eaten* before he came.
past perfect

I *will have eaten* before class.
future perfect

Remember that verb tenses indicate the time that an action occurs. Therefore, in order to show that actions take place at different times, different tenses must be used.

THE PRESENT PERFECT — The present perfect tense is used to express an action that occurred at an unspecified time in the past or an action that started in the past and continues into the present.

Has Ali ever *lived* in Kabul?
unspecified time in the past

Ali *has lived* in Kabul for four years.
continues into the present

IN ENGLISH

The present perfect is a compound tense formed with the auxiliary *have* in the present tense + the past participle of the main verb (see *What is an Auxiliary Verb?*, p. 99 and *What is a Participle?*, p. 95). In conversation *have* is usually shortened to *'ve*.

Have you *seen* Samir recently?
We*'ve seen* everyone but him.

IN ARABIC

In Arabic, most verbs form the present perfect with **qad** (قد) + the perfect tense of the verb. The particle **qad** (قد), known as "the perfective particle," changes the perfect tense to the present perfect (see *What is the Past Tense?*, p. 109).

*The professor **has come**.*
qad ḥaḍara l-'ustā<u>dh</u>-u. (قد حضر الاستاذ)

- **qad** (قد) : perfective particle
- **ḥaḍara** (حضرَ) *(he) came:* verb, 3rd pers. masc. sing., perfect
- **l-'ustā<u>dh</u>u** (الاستاذُ) *the professor:* noun, masc. sing. def., subj. of **ḥaḍara** (حضرَ) → nom.

The active participle of some verbs have present perfect meaning; for example, **dāris-u-n** (دارسٌ) *having studied.*

> 'anā **dāris-u-n** hā<u>dh</u>ā -l-dars-a(انا دارسٌ هذا الدرس) .
> *I **have studied** this lesson.*

As new Arabic verbs are introduced, make sure to learn the meaning of their active participle forms (see also pp. 96-7 and 121).

THE PAST PERFECT — The past perfect is used to express an action that was completed in the past before another action or event which also occurred in the past.

> She *remembered* that she *had forgotten* her keys.
> simple past (2) — past perfect (1)

Both actions 1 and 2 occurred in the past, but action 1 preceded action 2. Therefore, action 1 is in the past perfect.

IN ENGLISH

The past perfect is a compound tense formed with the auxiliary *have* in the past tense *(had)* + the past participle of the main verb: *I had walked, he had seen,* etc. In conversation *had* is often shortened to *'d.*

> They *had moved* before school *opened* in the fall.
> past perfect (1) — simple past (2)

Action 1 preceded action 2. Therefore, action 1 is in the past perfect.

IN ARABIC

The past perfect is a compound tense formed with the auxiliary verb **kāna**(كان) *he was (to be)* in the perfect tense + the perfective particle **qad** (قد) + the main verb in the perfect tense (see p. 109-10). Both the auxiliary verb and the main verb agree with the subject; for example: (1st pers. pl. perfect) **kun-nā + qad**(كنا قد)+ (1st pers. pl. perfect) **katab-nā** (كتبنا)→ *we had written.*

As in English, a verb is put in the past perfect in order to show that the action of that verb took place before the action of another verb in either the perfect or the past imperfect.

ENGLISH:	**Past perfect** **Past progressive**	**Simple past**	**Present**
ARABIC:	Past perfect	Perfect Past imperfect	Imperfect
	- 2	- 1	0
	x	x	x

TIME ACTION TAKES PLACE:
0 → now
- 1 → before 0
- 2 → before -1

Here are two examples.

*Huda **had finished** studying when **they arrived.***

past perfect -2 → action 1; simple past -1 → action 2

kān-at hudā **qad 'akmal-at** -l-dirāsat-a lammā **waṣal-ū**.
(كانت هُدى قد اكملت الدراسة لما وصلوا)

- **kānat** (كانت) *(she) was:* auxiliary verb, 3rd pers. fem. sing., perfect
- **hudā** (هُدى) *Huda:* proper noun, fem. sing. def., subj. of **kānat qad 'akmalat** (كانت قد اكملت)→ nom.
- **qad** (قد): perfective particle
- **'akmalat** (اكملت) *(she) finished:* main verb, 3rd pers. fem. sing., perfect
- **-l-dirāsata** (الدراسة) *studying:* gerund, fem. sing. def., obj. of **kānat qad 'akmalat** (كانت قد اكملت)→ acc.
- **lammā** (لما) *when:* subordinating conjunction
- **waṣalū** (وصلوا) *they arrived:* verb, 3rd pers. masc. pl., perfect

***I had eaten** so **I went** home.*

past perfect -2 → action 1; simple past -1 → action 2

kun-tu qad 'akal-tu fa-**raja**ᶜ**-tu** 'ilā -l-bayt-i.
(كنت قد اكلت فرجعت الى البيت)

- **kuntu** (كنت) *I was:* auxiliary verb, 1st pers. sing., perfect
- **qad** (قد): perfective particle
- **'akaltu** (اكلتُ) *I ate:* main verb, 1st pers. sing., perfect
- **fa-** (ف)*and so:* coordinating conjunction
- **raja**ᶜ**tu** (رجعتُ) *I returned:* main verb: 1st pers. sing., perfect
- **'ilā** (إلى) *to:* preposition
- **-l-bayti** (البيت) *the house:* noun, masc. sing. def., obj. of **'ilā** (إلى) → gen.

THE FUTURE PERFECT — The future perfect is used to express an action that will be completed in the future before another action or event in the future.

By the time we leave, he *will have finished.*

future event 2; future perfect 1

Both actions 1 and 2 will occur at some future time, but action 1 will be completed before action 2 takes place. Therefore, action 1 is in the future perfect tense.

IN ENGLISH

The future perfect is a compound tense formed with the auxiliary *have* in the future tense *(will have)* + the past participle of the main verb: *I will have walked, she will have gone.* In conversation *will* is often shortened to *'ll.*

The future perfect is often used following expressions such as *by then, by that time, by* + a date.

> By the end of the month, he*'ll have graduated.*
> By June, I*'ll have saved* enough to buy a car.

IN ARABIC

The future perfect is a compound tense composed of the auxiliary verb **kān-a** (كان) *he was (to be)* in the future tense + perfective particle **qad** (قد) + the main verb in the perfect tense (see p. 109-10). Both the auxiliary verb and the main verb agree with the subject; for example: (1st pers. pl. future) **sa-nakūn-u** + **qad**(سأكون قد) + (1st pers. pl. perfect) **katab-nā** (كتبنا) *we will have written.*

As in English, a verb is put in the future perfect in order to show that the action of that verb will take place before a specific future time.

Observe the sequence of future events expressed in the following time-line:

ENGLISH TENSE:	**Present**	**Future perfect**	**Future event**
ARABIC TENSE:	Imperfect	Future perfect	Future event
	0	1	2
	x	x	x

TIME ACTION TAKES PLACE:
0 → now
1 → after 0 and before 2
2 → after 0

I will have gone *before you begin.*

action 1 — action 2

sa-'akūn-u qad <u>dh</u>ahab-tu qabl-a 'an tabda'-ū.
(سأكون قد ذهبت قبل ان تبدأوا)

- **sa-** (س) *will:* future prefix
- **'akūnu** (أكونُ) *I will be:* auxiliary verb **kāna** (كان), 1st pers. sing., imperfect
- **qad** (قد)*:* perfective particle
- **<u>dh</u>ahabtu** (ذهبت) *I went:* main verb, 1st pers. sing., perfect
- **qabla 'an** (قبل ان) *before:* subordinating conjunction + subjunctive
- **tabda'ū** (تبدأوا) *you begin:* verb, 2nd pers. masc. pl., subjunctive

CHAPTER

36

WHAT ARE THE PROGRESSIVE TENSES?

The **PROGRESSIVE TENSES** are used to talk about actions that are in progress at a specific moment in time; they highlight the moment that an action takes place.

> Ali *is talking* on the phone.
> We *were trying* to start the car.

IN ENGLISH

The progessive tenses are composed of the auxiliary verb *to be* + the present participle of the main verb (see p. 95 in *What is a Participle?*). Notice that it is the tense of the auxiliary verb *to be* that indicates when the action of the main verb takes place.

> We *are leaving*.
> *to be* present tense — *to leave* present participle
> present progressive → right now

> We *were leaving*.
> *to be* past tense — *to leave* present participle
> past progressive → specific time in the past

IN ARABIC

In Arabic, depending on the verb, the progressive tenses are expressed in one of two ways: (a) the imperfect tense of some verbs or (b) the active participle of some verbs.

Some Arabic verbs have progressive meaning in both imperfect tense and the active participle, others have progressive meaning in one but not the other form and some verbs don't have progressive meaning at all. So that you will know which form to use, as new Arabic verbs are introduced be sure to learn the meaning of their imperfect and their active participle forms.

PRESENT PROGRESSIVE — The imperfect tense or the active participle, depending on the verb.

*Who **is using** the cell phone?*
man **yastaᶜmil-u** -l-mūbīl?
(من يستعمل الموبايل؟)
- **man** (من) *who?:* interrogative pronoun, subj. of **yastaᶜmilu** (يستعمل)
- **yastaᶜmilu** (يستعمل) *(he) uses:* verb, 3rd pers. masc. sing., imperfect
- **-l-mūbīl** (الموبايل) *the cell phone:* noun, masc. sing. def., obj. of **yastaᶜmilu** (يستعمل) → acc.

*Where [are] you **going**?*
'ilā 'ayna 'antum **dhāhib-ūna** (الى اين انتم ذاهبون؟)?
- **'ilā** (الى) *to:* preposition
- **'ayna** (اين) *where?:* interrogative adverb
- **'antum** (انتم) *you:* independent pronoun, 2nd pers. masc. pl., subj. in verbless sentence → nom.
- **dhāhibūna** (ذاهبون) *going:* active participle, masc. pl., predicate → nom. indef.

Past progressive — The auxiliary verb **kān-a** (كان) *he was (to be)* in the perfect tense + the main verb in the imperfect tense or the active participle, depending on the verb.

*The reporter **was conversing** with the minister.*
kān-a -l-murāsil-u **yataḥaddath-u** maᶜa -l-wazīr-i.
(كان المراسل يتحدث مع الوزير)
- **kāna** (كان) *(he) was:* auxiliary verb, 3rd pers. masc. sing., perfect
- **-l-murāsilu** (المراسل) *the reporter:* noun, masc. sing. def., subj. of **yataḥaddathu** (يتحدثُ)→ nom.
- **yataḥaddathu** (يتحدثُ) *he talks:* main verb, 3rd pers. masc. sing., imperfect
- **maᶜa** (مع) *with:* preposition
- **-l-wazīri** (الوزير) *the minister:* noun, masc. sing. def., obj. of **maᶜa** (مع) → gen.

*Why **was** the instructor **carrying** a stick?*
li-mādhā **kān-a** -l-mudarris-u **ḥāmil-an** ᶜaṣa-n?
(لماذا كان المدرس حاملا عصاً؟)
- **li-mādhā** (لماذا) *why?:* interrogative adverb
- **kāna** (كان) *(he) was:* auxiliary verb, 3rd pers. masc. sing., perfect
- **-l-mudarrisu** (المدرسُ) *the instructor:* noun, masc. sing. def., subj. of **kāna** (كان) → nom.
- **ḥāmilan** (حاملًا)*carrying:* active participle, masc. sing., predicate → acc. indef.
- **ᶜaṣan** (عصاً) *a stick:* noun, fem. sing., dir. obj. of **ḥāmilan** (حاملًا) → acc. indef.

CHAPTER

37

WHAT IS MEANT BY ACTIVE AND PASSIVE VOICE?

VOICE in the grammatical sense refers to the relationship between the verb and its subject. There are two voices, the **ACTIVE VOICE** and the **PASSIVE VOICE.**

ACTIVE VOICE — A sentence is said to be in the active voice when the subject is the performer of the action of the verb and the direct object is the receiver of the action (see *What is a Subject?*, p. 32, *What is a Verb?*, p. 84, and *What are Objects?*, p. 36). In this instance, the verb is called an **ACTIVE VERB.**

The president *signs* the agreement.
S V DO

The subject (S) performs the action of the verb (V) and the direct object (DO) is the receiver of the action.

PASSIVE VOICE — A sentence is said to be in the passive voice when the subject is the receiver of the action of the verb. The performer of the action, if it is mentioned, is introduced by the word "by" and is called the **AGENT**. In this instance, the verb is called a **PASSIVE VERB.**

The agreement *is signed* by the president.
S V agent

The subject is the receiver of the action of the verb and *by* introduces the agent, the performer of the action.

IN ENGLISH

The passive voice is expressed by the verb *to be* conjugated in the appropriate tense + the past participle of the main verb (see *What is a Participle?*, p. 95). The tense of the passive sentence is indicated by the tense of the verb *to be.*

The agreement ***is** signed* by the president.
present

The agreement ***was** signed* by the president.
past

The agreement ***will be** signed* by the president.
future

IN ARABIC

In Arabic, both the imperfect and the perfect tenses have active and passive voice. Unlike English that uses an auxiliary verb to make verbs passive, Arabic merely changes the vowel pattern of the active verb.

Imperfect passive — In the imperfect passive, the first vowel of the active imperfect subject prefix is changed from **-a-** to **-u-** and the following vowels of the stem are changed to **-a-**. The inflectional endings are the same as for the active verb.

VERB: **'akal-a** (أكَل) *he ate (to eat)*

ACTIVE VOICE	y**a**'k**u**l-u (يأكُل)	*he/it eats*
PASSIVE VOICE	y**u**'k**a**l-u (يؤْكَل)	*he/it is eaten*

VERB: **'istaqbal-a** (استقبَل) *he welcomed (to welcome)*

ACTIVE VOICE	y**a**staqb**i**l-u (يستقبِل)	*he welcomes*
PASSIVE VOICE	y**u**staqb**a**l-u (يستقبَل)	*he is welcomed*

Perfect passive — In the perfect passive, the stem vowel of the active verb changes to **-i-** and the preceding vowels in the word are all changed to **-u-**. The inflectional endings are the same as for the active verb.

VERB: **'akal-a** (أكَل) *he ate (to eat)*

ACTIVE	'**a**k**a**l-a (أكَل)	*he/it ate*
PASSIVE VOICE	'**u**k**i**l-a (أكِل)	*he/it was eaten*

VERB: **'i-staqbal-a** (استقبَل) *he welcomed (to welcome)*

ACTIVE VOICE	'**i**-st**a**qb**a**l-a (إستقبال)	*he welcomed*
PASSIVE VOICE	'**u**-st**u**qb**i**l-a (إستقبل)	*he was welcomed*

ACTIVE VOICE → PASSIVE VOICE

As in English, when changing an active sentence to the passive, the object of the active verb becomes the subject of the passive verb. In Arabic, this is reflected in a change of case: the accusative object of the active sentence becomes the nominative subject of the passive sentence.

Unlike English, however, the agent, i.e., the performer of the action of the verb, is not expressed in a passive sentence.

Here is an example of a sentence changed from the imperfect active to the imperfect passive.

Gibran ***is eating*** *the apple.*

Who is eating the apple?

Gibran → subject → performer of the action → active voice

jibrān-u **ya'kul-u** -l-tuffāḥat-a (جبران يأكلُ التفاحة).

- **jibrān-u** (جبران) *Gibran:* proper noun, masc. sing. def., subj. of **ya'kulu** (يأكل)→ nom.
- **ya'kulu** (يأكل) *(he) eats:* verb, 3rd pers. masc. sing., imperfect
- **-l-tuffāḥata** (التفاحة) *the apple:* noun, fem. sing. def., obj. of **ya'kulu** (يأكل) → acc.

The apple ***is being eaten*** *now [by Gibran].*

What is being eaten?

The apple → subject → recipient of verb *to eat*

'a-l-tuffāḥat-u **tu'kal-u** -l-'āna (التفاحة تؤكل الآن) .

- **'al-tuffāḥatu** (التفاحة) *the apple*: noun, fem. sing. def., subj. of **tu'kalu** (تؤكل) → nom.
- **tu'kalu** (تؤكل) *is eaten:* verb, 3rd pers. fem. sing., imperfect passive
- **-l-'āna** (الآن) *now:* adverb

Here is an example of a sentence changed from the perfect active to the perfect passive.

Hind ***ate*** *the apple.*

Who ate the apple?

Hind → subject → performer of the action → active voice

'akal-at hind-u-n -l-tuffāḥat-a.
(أكلت هند التفاحة)

- **'akalat** (أكلت) *(she) ate:* verb, 3rd pers. fem. sing., perfect
- **hindun** (هند) *Hind:* proper noun, fem. sing. def., subj. of **'akalat** (أكلت) → nom.
- **-l-tuffāḥata** (التفاحة) *the apple:* noun, fem. sing. def., obj. of **'akalat** (أكلت) → acc.

The apple ***was eaten*** *[by Hind].*

What was eaten?

The apple → subject → recipient of verb *to eat* → passive voice

'ukil-at -l-tuffāḥat-u (أُكِلت التفاحة) .

- **'ukilat** (أُكِلت) *(she) was eaten:* verb, 3rd pers. fem. sing., perfect passive
- **-l-tuffāḥatu** (التفاحة) *the apple:* noun, fem. sing. def., subj. of **'ukilat** (أُكِلت) → nom.

CHAPTER

38

WHAT IS MEANT BY MOOD?

MOOD in the grammatical sense is a termapplied to verbs and indicates the attitude of the speaker toward what he or she is saying.

Different moods serve different purposes. For instance, verb tenses which state a fact belong to one mood *(you are studying)* and the verb forms that give orders belong to another *(Study!)*. Some moods have multiple tenses, while others have only one tense.

You should recognize the names of moods so that you will know what your Arabic textbook is referring to when it uses these terms. You will learn when to use the various moods as you learn verbs and their tenses.

IN ENGLISH

Verbs can be in one of three moods:

1. **INDICATIVE MOOD** — The indicative mood is used to state facts or to ask questions. This is the most common mood and most of the verb forms that you use in everyday conversation belong to the indicative mood.

   Robert *studies* Arabic.
   present indicative

   Anita *was* here.
   past indicative

   They *will arrive* tomorrow.
   future indicative

2. **IMPERATIVE MOOD** — The imperative mood is used to give commands or orders. This mood is not divided into tenses (see p. 131).

   Robert, *study* your Arabic now!
   Anita, *be* home on time!

3. **SUBJUNCTIVE MOOD** — The subjunctive mood is used to express hypothetical, doubtful or subjective statements (see p. 128).

   The school requires that students *study* Arabic.
   I wish that Anita *were* here.
   The teacher recommends that he *do* his homework.

IN ARABIC

Verbs can be in one of four moods:

1. **INDICATIVE MOOD** — As in English, the indicative mood is the most common. It is the only mood that has more than one tense: the imperfect (**yaktub-u** (يكتبُ) *he writes)* and the perfect (**katab-a** (كتبَ) *he wrote).* It is the mood to use if you have no reason to use another mood.
2. **IMPERATIVE MOOD** — As in English, the imperative is used to give orders.
3. **SUBJUNCTIVE MOOD** — As in English, Arabic has a subjunctive mood. However, it is used more frequently than in English.
4. **JUSSIVE MOOD** — This mood assumes some of the functions of the English imperative mood and is used for negative forms of the perfect tense (see pp, 133-4 *What is the Imperative Mood?* and pp. 154-5 in *What are Affirmative, Negative, Declarative and Interrogative, Sentences?*).

The different moods are indicated by different suffixes. When there is no reference to mood in your textbook, you can assume that the tense belongs to the most common mood, the indicative.

CHAPTER

39

WHAT IS THE SUBJUNCTIVE MOOD?

The **SUBJUNCTIVE** is a mood used to express a wish, hope, uncertainty or other similar attitude toward a fact or an idea.

I wish he *were* here.
verb of wishing — subjunctive

The teacher insisted that the homework *be* neat.
verb of demanding — subjunctive

IN ENGLISH

The subjunctive verb form is difficult to recognize because it is similar to other forms of the verb.

INDICATIVE	SUBJUNCTIVE
He *reads* a lot. indicative present *to read*	The course requires that he *read* a lot. subjunctive (same as dictionary form)
I *am* in New York. indicative present *to be*	I wish I *were* in Marrakesh. subjunctive (same as past tense plural)

The subjunctive occurs most commonly in three kinds of sentences.

1. in contrary-to-fact statements (see *What are Conditional Sentences?*, p. 149)

   If I *were* in Europe now, I would go on to Marrakesh.
   subjunctive
   contrary-to-fact (speaker is not in Europe)

   If you *sang* better, you could go on TV.
   subjunctive
   contrary-to-fact (you do not sing that well)

2. in statements expressing a wish (also contrary-to-fact)

   I wish I *were* in Europe right now.
   subjunctive
   contrary-to-fact (speaker is not in Europe)

   I wish she *were* my teacher.
   subjunctive
   contrary-to-fact (she is not my teacher)

3. in clauses following verbs that ask, urge, demand, request or express necessity (see p. 146 in *What are Phrases, Clauses and Sentences?*).

She asked that he *be* early today.
request — subjunctive (instead of indicative *is*)

It is moved that the officers *be elected* annually.
request — subjunctive (instead of indicative *are elected*)

IN ARABIC

Unlike English, the subjunctive mood is very common in Arabic and its forms are easily recognizable. It is formed by changing the short **-u** suffix of the indicative to the short **–a** suffix and dropping the suffixes **-na** and **-ni** that follow long vowels.

VERB: **daras-a** (دَرَسَ) *he studied (to study)*

INDICATIVE:	'adrus-**u**	(أَدْرُسُ)	*I study*
SUBJUNCTIVE:	'adrus-**a**	(أدرسَ)	
INDICATIVE:	tadrusī-**na** **(fem. sing.)**	(تدرسين)	*you study*
SUBJUNCTIVE:	tadrusī	(تدرسي)	
INDICATIVE:	tadrusū-**na** **(masc. pl.)**	(تدرسون)	*you study*
SUBJUNCTIVE:	tadrusū	(تدرسوا)	
INDICATIVE:	yadrusā-**ni**	(يدرسان)	*they study*
SUBJUNCTIVE:	yadrusā	(يدرسا)	

The subjunctive occurs primarily after the conjunction **'an**(أن) *that* and words combined with it, such as **yajib-u 'an** (يجبُ أن) *it is necessary that.* Here is an example of the complete conjugation of **darasa-a** (دَرَسَ) in the sujunctive. Notice that the conjunction **'an** (أنْ) is included in the conjugation.

SINGULAR				
1st PERSON		'an 'adrus-**a**	(أنْ أدْرُسَ)	*that I study*
2nd PERSON	**(masc.)**	'an tadrus-**a**	(أنْ تدرسَ)	*that you study*
	(fem.)	'an tadrus-**ī**	(أنْ تدرسي)	*that you study*
3rd PERSON	**(masc.)**	'an yadrus-**a**	(أنْ يدرسَ)	*that he study*
	(fem.)	'an tadrus-**a**	(أنْ تدرسَ)	*that she study*
DUAL				
2nd PERSON		'an tadrus-**ā**	(أنْ تدرسا)	*that you study*
3rd PERSON	**(masc.)**	'an yadrus-**ā**	(أنْ يدرسا)	*that they study*
	(fem.)	'an tadrus-**ā**	(أنْ تدرسا)	*that they study*
PLURAL				
1st PERSON		'an nadrus-**a**	(أنْ ندرسَ)	*that we study*
2nd PERSON	**(masc.)**	'an tadrus-**ū**	(أنْ تدرسوا)	*that you study*
	(fem.)	'an tadrus-**na**	(أنْ تدرسن)	*that you study*
3rd PERSON	**(masc.)**	'an yadrus-**ū**	(أنْ يدرسوا)	*that they study*
	(fem.)	'an yadrus-**na**	(أنْ يدرسن)	*that they study*

English infinitives often correspond to an Arabic subjunctive. You can identify these infinitives by placing *in order to, it is necessary that, that* before the English verb; if the meaning does not change, then the Arabic equivalent is probably in the subjunctive. Here are some examples.

*He lives **to eat**.*
*He lives **in order to eat**.*
ya^{c}īsh-u **li-ya'kul-a** (يعيشُ لِيأْكلَ) .
- **ya^{c}īshu** (يعيشُ) *he lives:* verb, 3rd pers. masc. sing., imperfect
- **li-** (لِ) *in order that:* conjunction + subjunctive
- **ya'kula** (يأْكلَ) *he eat:* verb, 3rd pers. masc. sing., subjunctive

*I **must** go now.*
***It is necessary that I go** now.*
yajib-u **'an 'adhhab-a** -l-'āna (يجب أنْ أذهبَ الآنَ) .
- **yajibu** (يجب) *it is necessary:* verb, 3rd pers. masc. sing., imperfect
- **'an** (أن) *that:* conjunction + subjunctive
- **'adhhaba** (أذهبَ) *I go:* verb, 1st pers. sing., subjunctive
- **-l-'āna** (الآن) *now:* adverb

*We want him **to become** a doctor.*
*We want **that he become** a doctor.*
nurīd-u **'an yuṣbiḥ-a** ṭabīb-a-n (نريدُ أن يصبحَ طبيباً).
- **nurīdu** (نريدُ) *we want:* verb, 1st pers. pl., imperfect
- **'an** (أن) *that:* conjunction + subjunctive
- **yuṣbiḥa** (يصبحَ) *he become:* verb, 3rd pers. masc. sing., subjunctive
- **ṭabīban** (طبيباً) *a doctor:* noun, masc. sing., predicate after linking verb **yuṣbiḥa** (يصبحَ) → acc. indef.

CHAPTER 40

WHAT IS THE IMPERATIVE MOOD?

The **IMPERATIVE** is a verb mood used to give a person or persons a command.

The **AFFIRMATIVE IMPERATIVE** is an order to do something.

Come here!

The **NEGATIVE IMPERATIVE** is an order not to do something.

Don't come here!

IN ENGLISH

There are two types of command, depending on who is told to do, or not to do, something.

1. **DIRECT COMMAND** — When an order is given to one or more persons, the dictionary form of the verb is used.

AFFIRMATIVE IMPERATIVE	NEGATIVE IMPERATIVE
Answer the phone!	*Don't answer* the phone!
Clean your room!	*Don't clean* your room!
Speak softly!	*Don't speak* softly!

2. **INDIRECT COMMAND** — There are two types of indirect commands, each one requiring a different form.

- When an order is given to oneself as well as to others, the phrase "let's" (a contraction of *let us*) is used + the dictionary form of the verb.

AFFIRMATIVE IMPERATIVE	NEGATIVE IMPERATIVE
Let's leave!	*Let's not leave!*
Let's go!	*Let's not go*!

- When an order is given to someone to order a third party to do something, *have* or *make* is used.

AFFIRMATIVE IMPERATIVE	NEGATIVE IMPERATIVE
Make them *leave!*	*Don't make* them *leave.*
Have them *go*!	*Don't have* them *go*!

IN ARABIC

As in English, there are special verb forms to give commands. Unlike English, however, different forms and moods are used depending on whether the command is affirmative or negative.

AFFIRMATIVE COMMAND — An affirmative command is given in the **IMPERATIVE MOOD** which exists only in the 2nd person and is based on the imperfect. Here are three verbs to illustrate the various steps to form the imperative.

1. Take the 2nd person imperfect indicative form.

masc. sing.	→	tusakkiru (تسكّرُ)	*you close*
fem. sing.	→	taftaḥīna (تفْتحين)	*you open*
dual	→	tadrusāni (تدْرسان)	*you study*
masc. pl.	→	tadrusūna (تدْرسون)	*you study*

2. Suffixes — Delete any final **-u** or **-na** or **-ni** following a long vowel.

tusakkir~~u~~	→	tusakkir (تسكرْ)
taftaḥī~~na~~	→	taftaḥī (تفْتحي)
tadrusā~~ni~~	→	tadrusā (تدْرسا)
tadrusū~~na~~	→	tadrusū (تدرسوا)

3. Prefixes — Delete the prefix that identifies the subject (see *What is a Verb Conjugation?*, p. 90).

~~tu~~sakkir	→	sakkir (سكرْ)
~~ta~~ftaḥī	→	-ftaḥī (افْتحي)
~~ta~~drusā-	→	-drusā (ادْرسا)
~~ta~~drusū-	→	-drusū (ادْرسوا)

4. Number of consonants at beginning of stem.

- one consonant → form above is imperative

  sakkir! (سكرْ) *Close!*

  masc. sing.

- two consonants → add prefix helping vowel **'u-** or **'i-** depending on stem vowel → imperative form

  a) if stem vowel **-u-** → prefix **'u-**

  -dr**u**sā → **'u**-drusā (أدْرسا) *Study!*
  (دْرسا)
  dual

  -dr**u**sū → **'u**-drusū (أدرسوا) *Study!*
  (دْرسوا)
  masc. pl.

  b) if any other stem vowel → prefix **'i-**

  -ft**a**ḥī → **'i**-ftaḥī (افْتحي) *Open!*
  (فْتحي)
  fem. sing.

Here is a chart of the imperative of **daras-a** (درَسَ) *he studied (to study)* you can use as reference.

VERB: **daras-a** (درَسَ) *he studied (to study)*
Indicative 2nd pers. masc. sing.: **tadrus-u** (تدرسُ) *you study*
Delete **-u**: **tadrus-~~u~~** → **tadrus** (تدرس)
Delete prefix: **~~ta~~drus** → **-drus** (درس)
Stem: 2 consonants + vowel "u" → prefix **'u-**
Imperative 2nd pers. masc. sing.: **'u-drus** (أدْرُسْ) *(study!)*

SINGULAR			
2ND PERSON (masc.)	'u-drus	(أُدْرُسْ)	*Study!*
2ND PERSON (fem.)	'u-drus-**ī**	(أدرسي)	
DUAL	'u-drus-**ā**	(أدرسا)	
PLURAL			
2ND PERSON (masc.)	'u-drus-**ū**	(أدرسوا)	
2ND PERSON (fem.)	'u-drus-**na**	(أدرسن)	

The imperative mood is only used for direct affirmative commands; i.e., when the speaker tells a person directly to do something.

Write your name in the book.
|
'u-ktubī (أكتبي)

NEGATIVE COMMAND — A negative command is given in the **JUSSIVE MOOD** which exists in the 1st, 2nd and 3rd persons and is based on the subjunctive mood (see *What is the Subjunctive Mood?*, p. 128). To form the jussive simply delete the final **-a** inflection of the subjunctive, but not the "**a**" of the feminine plural endings. The jussive uses gender and number suffixes but has no mood suffix.

Here is a chart of the jussive of **daras-a** (دَرَسَ) *he studied (to study)* you can use as reference.

Subjunctive: 'adrus~~a~~ → 'adrus- (أدرس)

SINGULAR				
1ST PERSON		'adrus	(أدرسْ)	*(that) I study*
	(masc.)	tadrus	(تدرسْ)	*(that) you study*
	(fem.)	tadrus-**ī**	(تدرسي)	*(that) you study*
3RD PERSON	**(masc.)**	yadrus	(يدرسْ)	*(that) he study*
	(fem.)	tadrus	(تدرسْ)	*(that) she study*
DUAL				
2ND PERSON		tadrus-**ā**	(تدرسا)	*(that) you study*
3RD PERSON	**(masc.)**	yadrus-**ā**	(يدرسا)	*(that) they study*
	(fem.)	tadrus-**ā**	(تدرسا)	*(that) they study*
PLURAL				
1ST PERSON		nadrus	(ندرسْ)	*(that) we study*
2ND PERSON	**(masc.)**	tadrus-**ū**	(تدرسوا)	*that) you study*
	(fem.)	tadrus-**na**	(تدرسْنَ)	*(that) you study*
3RD PERSON	**(masc.)**	yadrus-**ū**	(يدرسوا)	*(that) they study*
	(fem.)	yadrus-**na**	(يدرسن)	*(that) they study*

The jussive form is used to give two types of commands::

1. A direct negative command → **lā** (لا) *not* + 2nd pers. jussive form

   ***Don't close** the door!*

   lā tusakkir (لا تُسكّرْ)

   jussive 2nd masc. sing. of **sakkara** (سكّر) *he closed (to close)*

2. An indirect command → **li-** (لِ) + appropriate person of jussive form

   - an order is given to do something with the speaker → **li-**(لِ)+ 1st person plural of jussive verb

     ***Let's close** the door.*

     speaker + others

     li-nusakkir (لِنُسكّرْ)

     jussive 1st pers. pl. **sakkara** (سكّر) *he closed (to close)*

   - an order is given to someone to order a third party to do something → **li-**(لِ)+ 3rd person jussive form

     ***Have him close** the door.*

     li-yusakkir (لِيُسكّرْ)

     jussive 3rd pers. sing. of **sakkara** (سكّر) *he closed (to close)*

The jussive mood is also used for the negative form of the perfect tense (see pp. 154-5 in *What are Declarative, Interrogative, Affirmative and Negative Sentences?).* Your textbook will also introduce you to other uses of the jussive mood.

CHAPTER 41

WHAT IS A PREPOSITION?

A **PREPOSITION** is a word that shows the relationship of a noun or pronoun to other words in the sentence.

prepositional phrase

Paul has an appointment *after* school.

preposition object of preposition

The noun or pronoun following the preposition is called the **OBJECT OF THE PREPOSITION.** The preposition plus its object is called a **PREPOSITIONAL PHRASE.**

IN ENGLISH

Prepositions normally indicate such things as location, manner, direction, or time.

- to show location

  Khartoum is *in* the Sudan.

- to show manner

  Ali answered *with* great care.

- to show direction

  Can we drive *from* Cairo *to* Benghazi?

- to show extent of time

  We lived in the Middle East *for* many years.

- to show accompaniment

  Suad went to Damascus *with* her family.

- to show agent

  This play was written *by* Tawfiq Al-Hakim.

Other frequently used prepositions are: *during, since, with, between, of, about.*

To help you recognize prepositional phrases, here is a story where the prepositional phrases are in *italics* and the preposition which introduces each phrase is in ***boldface.***

There are many stories ***in*** *the Arab World* ***about*** *Juha,* a mullah, that is, an expert ***in*** *Islamic law.* Juha is a wise savant, half the time wise and half the time ***on*** *the stupid side.* He is popular not only ***among*** *the Arabs* but also **in** *Turkish, Iranian and Kurdish cultures.* He was probably a historical figure, and they say that he requested that ***after*** *his death* he be buried ***in*** *a rectangular cemetery,* surrounded ***by*** *just three walls* ***with*** *a door* ***in*** *one* ***of*** *them,* a door ***with*** *a big lock.* He wanted to continue giving people pleasure even ***after*** *his death.*

IN ARABIC

In Arabic there are twelve prepositions: **bi-** (بِ) *in; by;* **li-** (لِ) *for, to;* **ka-** (كَ) *like, as;* **min** (مِن) *from;* **ᶜan** (عَن) *(away) from; about;* **fī** (في) *in;* **'ilā** (الى) *to;* **ᶜalā** (على) *on;* **ladā** (لَدى) *at;* **ladun** (لَدُن) *at;* **maᶜa** (مع) *with;* **ḥattā** (حتّى) *up to, as far as;* and **mun<u>dh</u>u** (مُنْذُ) *since.* Prepositions are particles; that is, they never change form. The prepositional phrase in Arabic consists of a preposition plus a noun or pronoun object in the genitive.

[Are] you going ***to*** *class now?*
hal 'anta <u>dh</u>āhib-u-n **'ilā** -l-ṣaff-i -l'āna?
(هل أنت ذاهبٌ إلى الصف الآن؟)

- **hal**:(هل) interrogative particle, changes statement to a question
- **'anta** (أنت) *you:* personal pronoun, 2nd pers. masc. sing., subj. in verbless sentence → nom.
- **<u>dh</u>āhibun** (ذاهبٌ) *going:* active participle of verb **<u>dh</u>ahaba** (ذهبَ) *he went (to go),* masc. sing., predicate → nom. indef.
- **'ilā** (إلى) *to:* preposition
- **-l-ṣaffi** (الصف) *the class:* noun, masc. sing. def., obj. of **'ilā** (إلى) → gen.
- **-l'āna** (الآن) *now:* adverb

The ball went ***behind*** *the house.*
<u>dh</u>ahab-at -l-kurat-u **'ilā warā'i** -l-bayt-i.
(ذهبت الكرةُ إلى وراء البيت)

- **<u>dh</u>ahabat** (ذهبت) *(she) went:* verb, 3rd pers. sing., perfect
- **-l-kuratu** (الكرةُ) *the ball:* noun, fem. sing. def., subj. of **<u>dh</u>ahabat** (ذهبت) → nom.
- **'ilā** (إلى) *to:* preposition
- **warā'i** (وراء) *behind:* noun-preposition, obj. of **'ilā** (إلى) → gen.
- **-l-bayti** (البيت) *the house:* noun, masc. sing. def., obj. of **warā'i** (وراء) → gen.

PREPOSITION VS. NOUN USED AS A PREPOSITION

In addition to the true prepositions listed above, many Arabic nouns function as prepositions. Arabic grammars call them "noun-prepositions," "pseudo-prepositions" or just "prepositions." A noun-preposition is easily distinguished from a true preposition since it is any word that is defined as a "preposition" and ends with **-a** (except **ka** (كَ) - *like* and **maᶜa** (مع) *with*).

It is important that you distinguish between true prepositions and noun-prepositions. True prepositions never change form whereas noun-prepositions change from the accusative to the genitive if they become the object of another preposition. Here are examples of noun-prepositions: **'amām-a** (أمامَ) *at the front of, before* and **ba^c^d-a** (بعدَ) *after.*

The professor [is] standing ***in front of*** *the class.*
'al-'ustā<u>dh</u>u wāqif-u-n **'amām-a** -l-ṣaff-i.
(الاستاذ واقفٌ أمام الصف)

- **'al-'ustā<u>dh</u>u** (الاستاذ) *the professor:* noun, masc. sing. def., subj. in verbless sentence → nom.
- **wāqifun** (واقفٌ) *standing:* active participle, masc. sing., predicate → nom. indef.
- **'amāma** (أمامَ) *in front of:* noun-preposition
- **-l-ṣaffi** (الصفِ) *the class:* noun, masc. sing. def., obj. of **'amāma** (أمامَ)→ gen.

I'll see you ***after*** *class.*
sa'arā-ka **ba^c^d-a** -l-ṣaff-i (سأراك بعد الصف) .

- **sa** (سَ)- *will:* future prefix
- **'arā** (أرا) *I see:* verb, 1st pers. sing., imperfect
- **-ka** (كَ) *you:* personal pronoun, 2nd pers. masc. sing., obj. of **'arā** (أرا)→ acc.
- **ba^c^da** (بعدَ) *after:* noun-preposition
- **-l-ṣaffi** (الصفِ) *class:* noun, masc. sing. def., obj. of **ba^c^da** (بعدَ)→ gen.

CAREFUL — Prepositions are tricky. When you memorize Arabic prepositions pay special attention to their meaning and use. In addition, English prepositions have a range of meanings that often match more than one Arabic preposition. For example, the English preposition *with* has many meanings and a different Arabic equivalent for each one.

I went *with* John to the concert.
in the company of → **ma^c^a** (معَ)

I signed it *with* my own pen.
using → **bi-** (بِ)

She left her books *with* her sister.
at the place of → **^c^ind-a** (عندَ)

CHAPTER **42**

WHAT IS AN ADVERB?

An **ADVERB** is a word that describes a verb, an adjective, or another adverb. It indicates manner, degree, time, place, etc.

Karim drives *well.*
verb adverb

The house is *very* big.
adverb adjective

The girl ran *too quickly.*
adverb adverb

IN ENGLISH

There are different types of adverbs, such as:

- **ADVERB OF MANNER** — answers the question *how?* Adverbs of manner are the most common and they are easy to recognize because they end with *-ly*.

  Fatima sings *beautifully.*

  Beautifully describes the verb *sings;* tells you how Fatima sings.

- **ADVERB OF TIME** — answers the question *when?*

  We expect he will arrive *soon.*

- **ADVERB OF PLACE** — answers the question *where?*

  Hang your coat *there.*

IN ARABIC

In Arabic, adverbs typically end in **–u**; for example, **baʿdu** (بعدُ) *later*; **fawqu** (فوقُ) *above*; **taḥtu** (تحتُ) *below*; **faqaṭ** (فقطْ) *only* and **'ayḍan** (أيضاً) *also.* Adverbs are particles; that is, they never change form.

In addition to the true adverbs listed above, many Arabic nouns and adjectives in the accusative case indefinite and prepositional phrases function as adverbs: **ṣarāḥat-a-n** (صراحةً) *frankly* (from the noun **ṣarāḥat-u-n** (صراحةٌ) *candor),* **qarīb-a-n** (قريباً) *soon* (from the adjective **qarīb-u-n** (قريبٌ) *near)* **bi-surʿat-i-n** (بسرعةٍ) *quickly.* Your textbook will introduce you to other expressions that serve as adverbs.

CAREFUL — Some English words can function as an adverb or as an adjective. It is important to distinguish between the two parts of speech because in Arabic different words and different rules will apply. To distinguish between an adverb and an adjective, identify the part of speech the word modifies: if the word modifies a noun it is an adjective; if it modifies a verb, an adjective, or an adverb it is an adverb.

Nadia learns ***fast.***

modifies verb *learns* → adverb

bi-surᶜat-in (بسرعةٍ)

prepositional phrase

Nadia is a ***fast*** *learner.*

modifies noun *learner* → adjective

sarīᶜat-u-n (سريعةٌ)

attributive adjective

He swims ***well.***

modifies verb *swims* → adverb

ḥasan-a-n (حَسنًا)

acc. indef. adjective

I am very ***well,*** *thank you .*

modifies pronoun *I* → adjective

bi-khayr-i-n (بخيرٍ)

prepositional phrase

CHAPTER 43

WHAT IS A CONJUNCTION?

A **CONJUNCTION** is a word that links two or more words or groups of words.

Ahmad *and* Zayd always study together.
conjunction

I don't want apples *or* oranges.
conjunction

They played cards *until* we arrived.
conjunction

IN ENGLISH

There are two kinds of conjunctions: coordinating and subordinating.

COORDINATING CONJUNCTIONS — Coordinating conjunctions joins words, phrases and clauses that are equal in construction; it coordinates elements of equal rank (see *What are Phrases, Clauses and Sentences?*, p. 145). The major coordinating conjunctions are *and, but, or* and *nor.*

good *or* evil
word word

over the river *and* through the woods
phrase phrase

The sea was rough, *but* the ship was well built.
main clause main clause

SUBORDINATING CONJUNCTIONS — Subordinating conjunctions joins a main clause and a dependent clause called a **SUBORDINATE CLAUSE.** Common subordinating conjunctions are *before, after, since, although, because, if, unless, that, so that, while* and *when.*

main clause subordinate clause
I'll arrange the furniture, *if* you will help me.
subordinating conjunction

subordinate clause — main clause

Although the sea was rough, the passengers felt safe.

subordinating conjunction

main clause — subordinate clause

They stopped the game *because* the guests had come.

subordinating conjunction

main clause — subordinate clause

We know *that* they will meet the deadline.

subordinating conjunction

Notice that the subordinate clause may come either at the beginning of the sentence or after the main clause.

IN ARABIC

Arabic also has coordinating and subordinating conjunctions. Arabic conjunctions may be single words (**lākin** (لكن) *but*, **'in** (إن) *if*), phrases (**maᶜa 'anna** (مع أنَّ) *although*, **bi-mā'anna** (بما أنَّ) *in asmuch as*), or single syllables (**wa-** (وَ)*and*, **li-**(لِ) *in order that*) prefixed to the following word.

Coordinating conjunctions — Coordinating conjunctions are followed by verbs in the indicative mood. Common coordinating conjunctions are **wa-**(وَ) *and*, **fa-**(فَ) *and so*, **'aw** (أوْ) *or* and **thumma** (ثمَّ) *and then.*

Zaynab ***and*** *Nabila came together.*
'at-at zaynab-u **wa**-nabīlat-u maᶜan (اتت زينبُ ونبيلةُ معاً).

- **'atat** (اتت) *(she) came:* verb, 3rd pers. fem., verb precedes its subj. → sing., perfect,
- **zaynabu** (زينبُ) *Zaynab:* proper noun, fem. sing. def., subj. of **'atat** (اتت) → nom.
- **wa-** (وَ) *and:* coordinating conjunction joining two proper nouns [Zaynab and Nabila]
- **nabīlatu** (نبيلةُ) *Nabila*: proper noun, fem. sing. def., subj. of **'atat** (اتت) → nom.
- **maᶜan** (معاً) *together:* adverb

I studied ***and then*** *I went to bed.*
daras-tu **thumma** nim-tu (درستُ ثم نمت) .

- **darastu** (درستُ) *I studied:* verb, 1st pers. sing., perfect
- **thumma** (ثمّ) *and then:* coordinating conjunction joining two main clauses *[I studied + I went to bed]*
- **nimtu** (نمت) *I slept:* perfect verb, 1st pers. sing., perfect

SUBORDINATING CONJUNCTIONS — Subordinating conjunctions fall into two groups: those that are followed by a verb in the indicative mood and those that take the subjunctive mood (see *What is the Subjunctive Mood?*, p. 128).

Here are examples of subordinating conjunctions that are followed by a verb in the indicative mood or a verbless sentence.

- **'anna** (ان) *that, the fact that,* **li'anna** (لأن) *because,* subordinating conjunctions followed by a noun or pronoun subject in the accusative

*I know **that** they'll come right away.*
'aʿrif-u **'anna**-hum sa-ya't-ūna ḥāl-a-n.(اعرف انهم سيأتون حالاً)
. **'aʿrifu** (اعرفُ) *I know:* verb, 1st pers. sing., imperfect
. **'anna** (ان) *that*: subordinating conjunction + indicative mood
. **-hum** (هم) *they:* personal pronoun, 3rd pers. masc. pl, subj. of **'anna** (ان) → acc.
. **sa-** (س) *will:* future prefix
. **ya'tūna** (يأتون) *(they) come:* verb, 3rd pers. masc. pl., imperfect
. **ḥālan** (حالاً) *immediately:* adverb

*Wait a bit **because** breakfast [is] coming now.*
'i-ntaḍhir qalīl-a-n **li'anna** -l-fuṭūr-a qādim-u-n -l-'āna.
(انتظر قليلا لأن الفطور قادم الآن)
. **'intaḍhir** (انتظر) *wait!:* verb, 2nd pers. masc. sing., imperative
. **qalīlan** (قليلاً) *a little:* adverb
. **li'anna** (لأن) *because:* subordinating conjunction + indicative mood
. **-l-fuṭūra** (الفطور) *breakfast:* noun, masc. sing. def., subj. of **li'anna** (لأن) → acc.
. **qādimun** (قادمٌ) *coming:* active participle, masc. sing., predicate in verbless sentence → nom. indef.
. **-l-'āna** (الآن) *now:* adverb

*We know you [**are**] from Khartoum.*
naʿrif-u **'anna**-ki min -l-khurtumi (نعرف انك من الخرطوم) .
. **naʿrif-u** (نعرف) *we know:* verb, 1st pers. pl., imperfect
. **'anna** (ان) *that:* subordinating conjunction + indicative mood
. **-ki** (كِ) *you:* suffixed pronoun, 2nd pers. fem. sing. subject of **'anna** (ان) → acc.
. **min** (من) *from:* preposition
. **-l-khurtumi** (الخرطوم) *Khartoum:* noun, fem. sing. def. obj. of **min** (من) → gen.

Here are examples of subordinating conjunctions that are followed by a verb in the subjunctive mood.

*You **must** be ready.*
yajib-u **'an** takūn-a jāhiz-a-n (يجب ان تكونَ جاهزًا).
. **yajibu** (يجب) *it is necessary:* verb, 3rd pers. masc. sing., imperfect
. **'an** (ان) *that:* subordinating conjunction + subjunctive
. **takūna** (تكونَ) *you be:* linking verb, 2nd pers. masc. sing., subjunctive
. **jāhizan** (جاهزًا) *ready:* adjective, masc. sing., predicate of **takūna** (تكونَ) → acc. indef.

*You must work hard **to become** a doctor.*
ᶜalay-ka **'an** takūn-a mujtahid-a-n **li-tuṣbiḥ-a** ṭabīb-a-n.
(عليك أن تكون مجتهدًا لتصبحَ طبيبًا)

- **ᶜalay** (علي) - (form of ᶜ**alā** (على) with suffix): *on:* preposition
- **-ka** (كَ) *you:* personal pronoun, 2nd pers. masc. sing., obj. of ᶜ**alay** (علي) - → gen.
- **'an** (أن) *that:* subordinating conjunction + subjunctive
- **takūna** (تكون) *you be:* linking verb, 2nd pers. masc. sing., subjunctive
- **mujtahidan** (مجتهدًا) *hard working:* adjective, masc. sing., predicate of **takūna** (تكون) → acc. indef.
- **li** (لِ)- *in order that:* subordinating conjunction + subjunctive
- **tuṣbiḥa** (تصبحَ) *you become:* linking verb, 2nd pers. masc. sing., subjunctive
- **ṭabīban** (طبيبًا) *a doctor:* noun, masc. sing., predicate of **tuṣbiḥa** (تصبحَ)→ acc. indef.

Your textbook and dictionary will tell you which conjunctions are followed by a verb in the subjunctive mood.

CAREFUL

1. The conjunction *that* has two equivalents in Arabic depending on its meaning.

   - *(the fact) that* → **'anna**(أنَّ) + indicative

     *I know **[that] you will help** them.*
     'aᶜrif-u **'anna**-kum **sa-tusāᶜid-ūna**-hum.
     (أعرفُ انكم ستساعدونهم)

     - **'aᶜrifu** (أعرفُ) *I know:* verb, 1st pers. sing., imperfect
     - **'anna** (أنَّ) *that:* subordinating conjunction + indicative
     - **-kum** (كم) *you:* personal pronoun, 2nd pers. masc. pl, subj. of **'anna** (أنَّ) → acc.
     - **sa** (س) - *will:* future prefix
     - **tusāᶜidūna** (تساعدونَ) *you help:* verb, 2nd pers. masc. pl., imperfect
     - **-hum** (هم) *them:* personal pronoun, 2nd pers. masc. pl., object of **tusāᶜidūna** (تساعدونَ) → acc.

   - *(it is required) that* → **'an** (أن) + subjunctive

     *I want **you to help** them.*
     *I want **that you help** them.*
     'urīd-u-kum **'an tusāᶜid-ū**-hum (أريدكم ان تساعدوهم).

     - **'urīdu** (أريدُ) *I want:* verb, 1st pers. sing., imperfect
     - **-kum** (كم) *you:* personal pronoun, 2nd pers. masc. pl., obj. of **'urīdu** (أريدُ) → acc.
     - **'an** (أن) that: subordinating conjunction + subjunctive
     - **tusāᶜidū** (تساعدو) *you help:* verb, 2nd pers. masc. pl., subjunctive
     - **-hum** (هم) *them:* personal pronoun, 3rd pers. masc. pl., obj. of **tusāᶜidū** (تساعدو) → acc.

2. Some English words can function as a conjunction or as a preposition. It is important to distinguish between the two parts of speech because in Arabic different words and different rules will apply. To distinguish between a conjunction and a preposition, identify the group of words being introduced: if the word introduces a clause it is a conjunction; if it introduces a phrase it is a preposition.

clause

The session ended ***before*** *they arrived.*

conjunction

qabla 'an (قبل أنْ)

prepositional phrase

The session ended ***before*** *his arrival.*

preposition

qabl-a (قبلَ)

CHAPTER 44

WHAT ARE PHRASES, CLAUSES AND SENTENCES?

Groups of words in a sentence are classified according to the parts of speech they contain. Sentences are classified according to the type of clauses they contain.

WHAT IS A PHRASE?

A phrase is a sequence of two or more words that function as a unit in a sentence. The focus of the unit, i.e., the essential word in the phrase, is called the **HEAD** of the phrase. The other words in the phrase, called **MODIFIERS**, give additional information about the head.

There are various types of phrases identified by the part of speech of the head of the phrase.

There are various types of phrases identified by the part of speech of the head of the phrase.

IN ENGLISH

NOUN PHRASE — noun + modifier(s)

The Constitution is *an important legal* ***document***.
The sage is *a* ***man*** *famous for his wisdom.*

ADJECTIVE PHRASE — adjective + modifier(s)

The young man was ***wise*** *beyond his years.*
Sinbad was *extremely* ***resourceful.***

DEMONSTRATIVE PHRASE — demonstrative pronoun + noun

This *book* is mine; whose are ***those*** *books?*
These *questions* are impossible.

PREPOSITIONAL PHRASE — preposition + noun or pronoun object

Sharif fell asleep ***during*** *the lecture.*
The lecture was boring, so Muna left ***with*** *him.*

VERB PHRASE — verb + words to specify a particular meaning of the verb

The students ***see*** the blackboard. *[to look at]*
We'll ***see to*** it. *[take care of]*

PARTICIPIAL PHRASE — participle + objects + modifiers

They came ***running*** *at full speed.*
"I'm not sure," he said, ***writing*** *on the blackboard.*

GERUND PHRASE — gerund (+ subject) (+ object) + (modifier)

We appreciate *your **coming** early.*
***Smoking** anything at all* is prohibited.

INFINITIVE PHRASE — infinitive (+ object) + modifier(s)

You don't want him ***to lose** the race.*
No, he wants ***to win** convincingly.*

IN ARABIC

As in English, Arabic phrases are identified by the part of speech of the head. Consult your textbook for the structure and agreement of words within each type of phrase.

WHAT IS A CLAUSE?

IN ENGLISH

A clause is a group of words containing at least a subject and a conjugated verb agreeing with that subject; it can also contain a variety of modifiers, objects of the verb, etc. There are two kinds of clauses, main and subordinate clauses:

MAIN (INDEPENDENT) CLAUSE — A main clause expresses the central idea of the sentence. If it were taken out of the sentence it could stand alone as a complete sentence.

Shafiq majored in ancient history when he was in college.
(Shafiq: subject; majored: verb; history: object)

SUBORDINATE (DEPENDENT) CLAUSE — A subordinate clause modifies the meaning of the main clause. If it were taken out of a sentence it could not stand alone because it begins with a subordinating conjunction (see *What are Conjunctions?*, p. 140).

(subordinate clause: *When Shafiq was in college*; main clause: he majored in ancient history)
When Shafiq was in college, he majored in ancient history.
(When: subordinating conjunction)

IN ARABIC

Like English, Arabic has main and subordinate clauses. Unlike English where all clauses must have a subject and a verb, Arabic has two kinds of clauses.

VERBAL SENTENCE — Although it is a "clause," Arabic grammars refer to a clause with a subject and a verb as a **VERBAL SENTENCE**.

The women students want *to study medicine.*
'a-l-ṭālibāt-u yurid-na dirāsat-a -l-ṭibb-i.
(الطالباتُ يردن دراسة الطب)

- **'a-l-ṭālibātu** (الطالباتُ) *the women students:* noun, fem. pl. def., subj. of **yuridna** (يردن) → nom.
- **yuridna** (يردن) *(they) want:* verb, 3rd pers. fem. pl., imperfect
- **dirāsata** (دراسة) *to study:* verbal noun, fem. sing., 1st term in gen. construct → def., obj. of **'yuridna** (يردن) → acc.
- **-l-ṭibbi** (الطب) *medicine:* noun, masc. sing. def., 2nd term in gen. construct → gen.

VERBLESS (EQUATIONAL) SENTENCE — Although it is a "clause," Arabic grammars refer to a clause without a verb as a **VERBLESS SENTENCE.** A clause without a verb results from the fact that Arabic does not express the affirmative of the verb *to be* in the present tense (see *What is the Present Tense?*, p. 106) and p. 147 in *What are Affirmative, Negative... Sentences?*).

The director's name [is] Mr. Khayruddin.
'i-smu -l-mudīr-i -l-sayyid-u khayr-u -l-dīn-i.
(اسم المدير السيد خير الدين)

- **'i-smu** (اسم) *the name:* noun, masc. sing., 1st term of gen. construct → def., subj. of verbless sentence → nom.
- **-l-mudīri** (المدير) *the director:* noun, masc. sing. def., 2nd term of gen. construct → gen.
- **-l-sayyidu** (السيد) *Mr.:* noun, masc sing. def., subj. in verbless sentence → nom.
- **khayru -l-dīni** (خير الدين) *Khayruddin:* proper noun, masc. sing. def., agrees with **l-sayyidu** (السيد) → nom.

WHAT IS A SENTENCE?

IN ENGLISH

There are different types of sentences.

SIMPLE SENTENCE — A simple sentence consists of one main clause with no subordinate clause.

Rashid spoke Arabic.
subject — verb — object

COMPOUND SENTENCE — A compound sentence consists of two or more main clauses joined by coordinating conjunctions (see *What is a Conjunction?*, p. 140).

[main clause: He studied Arabic] *and* [main clause: he resided in Tunis.]
and = coordinating conjunction

Complex sentence — A complex sentence consists of a main clause with one or more subordinate clauses.

main clause / subordinate clause

He lived in Egypt, *although* he didn't know Arabic.

subordinating conjunction

IN ARABIC

As in English, Arabic identifies the same three types of sentences.

CAREFUL — While the English relative pronoun introduces a subordinate claue, the Arabic relative pronoun is not part of a clause, but merely serves to link two main clauses (see pp. 79-80 in *What is a Relative Pronoun?*).

CHAPTER
45

WHAT ARE CONDITIONAL SENTENCES?

Conditional sentences are sentences stating that if a certain condition exists then a certain result can be expected.

condition / result

If he wins this race, it will be a suprise.

If I were you, I would accept the offer.

IN ENGLISH

Conditional sentences are complex sentences consisting of two clauses (see p. 146 in *What are Phrases, Clauses and Sentences?*).

- **Condition** — The subordinate clause, usually introduced by *if* or *unless.*
- **Result** — The main clause which is the result of the condition above.

The result clause can precede the condition clause.

result / condition

It will be a suprise if he wins this race.
I would accept the offer, if I were you.

There are two types of conditional sentences.

1. **Possible condition** — The condition may be true or realizable. It can take place in the present, past or future.
   - **present time** — The verbs in the condition and result clauses are in the present tense.

     If you *say* this, you *are* mistaken.
     (*say*: present; *are*: present)

   - **past time** — The verbs in the condition and result clauses are in the past tense.

     If you *said* this, you *were* mistaken.
     (*said*: past; *were*: past)

   - **future time** — The verb in the condition clause is in the present tense (a future time implied, see p. 113) and the verb in the result clause is in the future tense.

     If you *say* this, you *will be* mistaken.
     (*say*: present; *will be*: future)

2. **Contrary-to-fact statement** — The condition is not true or there is no possibility of its being realized. These statements can only be made about the present or the past.
   - **present time** — The verb in the condition clause is in the subjunctive mood (see *What is the Subjunctive Mood?*, p. 128) and the verb in the result clause is *would* + the dictionary form of the verb.

     If I *were* you, I *would accept* the offer.

     subjunctive — *would* + dictionary form

   - **past time** — The verb in the condition clause is in the past perfect and the verb in the result clause is *would have* + the past participle of the verb (see p. 118 in *What is the Past Perfect?* and *What is a Participle?*, p. 95).

     If I *had been* you, I *would have accepted* the offer.

     past perfect — *would have* + past participle

IN ARABIC

Unlike English which uses "if" to introduce all condition clauses, Arabic uses different words for "if" depending on the possibility of realizing the condition. Also, regardless of the English tenses, Arabic uses the perfect tense in both the condition and result clauses.

1. **Possible condition** — The condition clause is introduced by **'in** (إن) *if* (50% possibility of condition being realized) or **'idhā** (إذا) *if* (more than 50% possibility of condition being realized).
   - **present or future time** — The verbs in the condition and result clauses are in the perfect tense.

     If you go, I will go with you.
     'in dhahab-ta, dhahab-tu ma^{c}a-ka (إن ذهبتَ، ذهبتُ معك).
     'idhā dhahab-ta, dhahab-tu ma^{c}a-ka. (إذا ذهبت، ذهبت معك)

     - **'in /'idhā** (إن) *if:* particle for possible condition
     - **dhahabta** (ذهبتَ) *you went:* verb, 2nd pers. masc. sing., perfect
     - **dhahabtu** (ذهبتُ) *I went:* verb, 1st pers. sing., perfect
     - **ma^{c}a** (مع) *with:* preposition
     - **-ka** (كَ) *you:* personal pronoun, 2nd pers. masc. sing., obj. of **ma^{c}a** (مع) → gen.

   - **past time** — A condition that might have been possible in the past → **'in kān-a** (إن كان) + **qad** (قد) + main verb in perfect tense.

If you saw the movie, then how did you like it?
'in kun-ta qad shāhad-ta -l-fīlm-a fa-hal 'a^cjaba-ka?
(ان كنتَ قد شاهدتَ الفيلمَ فهل أعجبك؟)

- **'in** (إن) *if:* particle for possible condition
- **kunta** (كنتَ) *you were:* auxiliary verb, 2nd pers. masc. sing., perfect
- **qad** (قد): perfective particle
- **shāhadta** (شاهدتَ) *you saw:* main verb, 2nd pers. masc. sing., perfect
- **-l-fīlma** (الفيلمَ) *the movie:* noun, masc. sing. def., obj. of **shāhadta** (شاهدتَ) → acc.
- **fa** (ف)- *then:* conjunction
- **hal** (هل) : interrogative particle, turns statement to question
- **'a^cjaba** (أعجب) *he pleased:* main verb, 3rd pers. masc. sing., perfect
- **-ka** (كَ) *you:* personal pronoun, 2nd pers. masc. sing., obj. of **'a^cjaba** (أعجبَ) → acc.

Consult your textbook for variations on this structure.

2. **CONTRARY-TO-FACT STATEMENT** — The condition may refer to present or past time. The condition clause is introduced by **law** (لو) *if* and the result clause is introduced by **la-** (لأ) *indeed.*

■ **present time** — The verbs in the condition and result clauses are in the perfect tense.

If I were in your place, I would go immediately.
law kun-tu makān-a-ka **la-**dhahab-tu fawr-a-n.
(لو كنتُ مكانَك لذهبت فوراً)

- **law** (لو) *if:* particle of unreal condition
- **kuntu** (كنتُ) *I was:* verb, 1st pers. sing., perfect
- **makāna** (مكانَ) *place:* noun, masc. sing. def., noun used as expression of time → acc.
- **-ka** (كَ) *you:* personal pronoun, 2nd pers. masc. sing., obj. of **makāna** (مكانَ) → acc.
- **la-** (لَ) *indeed:* emphatic particle
- **dhahabtu** (ذهبت) *I went:* verb, 1st pers. sing., perfect
- **fawran** (فوراً) *immediately:* adverb

■ **past time** — The verbs in the condition and the result clauses are in the past perfect tense.

If you had gone, I would have gone with you.
law kun-ta **qad** dhahab-ta, **la-**kun-tu qad dhahab-tu ma^ca-ka (لو كنت قد ذهبت، لكنتُ قد ذهبت معك) .

- **law** (لو) *if:* particle of unreal condition
- **kunta** (كنتَ) *you were:* auxiliary verb, 2nd pers. masc. sing., perfect
- **qad** (قد) : perfective particle
- **dhahabta** (ذهبتَ) *you went:* main verb, 2nd pers. masc. sing., perfect
- **la** (لَ) - *indeed:* emphatic particle
- **kuntu** (كنتُ) *I was:* auxiliary verb, 1st pers. sing., perfect

- **qad** (قد) : perfective particle
- **dhahabtu** (ذهبت) *I went:* main verb, 1st pers. sing., perfect
- **maʿa** (مع) *with:* preposition
- **-ka** (كَ) *you:* personal pronoun, masc. sing., obj. of **maʿa** (مع) . → gen.

Consult your textbook for variations on these structures.

CAREFUL — There are three equivalents for the English *if*, make sure that you establish its precise meaning so that you can choose the appropriate Arabic equivalent.

- **'in** → (إن) *if, if it is/should be the case*
  'in katab-ta la-hā (إن كتبتَ لها)
  *If you write her/***if** *you should write her*
- **'idhā** → (إذا) *if, when*
  'idhā katab-ta la-hā (إذا كتبتَ لها)
  If you (ever) write her
- **law** → (لو) *if, if it were the case that*
  law katab-ta lahā (لو كتبتَ لها)
  If you were to write her, **if** *you wrote her*

CHAPTER 46

WHAT ARE AFFIRMATIVE, NEGATIVE, DECLARATIVE AND INTERROGATIVE SENTENCES?

A sentence can be classified as to whether it is making a statement or asking a question and as to whether it is using a negative word or not.

An **AFFIRMATIVE SENTENCE** makes a statement without a negative word such as *not, never, nobody* and *nothing.*

Kurdish is an Iranian language.

A **NEGATIVE SENTENCE** makes a statement with a negative word such as *not, never, nobody* and *nothing.*

Kurdish is *not* Semitic.

A **DECLARATIVE SENTENCE** is a sentence that makes a statement.

Arabic is a Semitic language.

An **INTERROGATIVE SENTENCE** is a sentence that asks a question.

Is Turkish a Semitic language?

AFFIRMATIVE AND NEGATIVE

IN ENGLISH

An affirmative sentence can be made negative in one of two ways:

- by adding *not* after auxiliary verbs or modals (see *What are Auxiliary Verbs?*, p. 99)

Affirmative	Winds *are* blowing.
Negative	Winds *are not* blowing.
Affirmative	May *will* tell you.
Negative	May *will not* tell you.

Frequently, the word *not* is attached to the verb and the letter "o" is replaced by an apostrophe: *is not* → *isn't; cannot* → *can't; will not* → *won't.*

- by using the auxiliary verb *to do* + *not* + the dictionary form of the main verb

Affirmative	Practice *makes* perfect.
Negative	Practice *does not* make perfect.

present

Affirmative I *swam in* the Red Sea.
Negative I *did not* swim in the Red Sea.
past

Frequently, *do, does,* or *did* is contracted with *not: do not → don't; does not → doesn't; did not → didn't.*

IN ARABIC

In Arabic the negative used depends on the type of sentence and the tense of the verb to be negated.

Present — lā (لا) *not* + verb in the imperfect

Affirmative ***He works** in the libary.*
yaᶜmal-u fī -l-maktabat-i (يعمل في المكتبة).
imperfect

Negative ***He doesn't work** in the library.*
lā yaᶜmal-u fī -l-maktabat-i (لا يعمل في المكتبة).
lā (لا) + imperfect

Future — sawfa lā (سوف لا) *will not* + verb in the imperfect or **lan** (لن) *will never, will not* + verb in subjunctive mood

Affirmative ***We'll see** you tomorrow.*
sa-narā-kum g͟hadan (سنراكم غداً) .
imperfect

Negative ***We won't see** you tomorrow.*
sawfa lā narā-kum g͟hadan (سوف لا نراكم غدا).
sawfa lā (سوف لا)+ imperfect

Affirmative ***We'll leave** tomorrow.*
sa-nusāfir-u g͟hadan (سنسافر غداً).
indicative mood

Negative ***We'll** never **leave.***
lan nusāfir-a 'abadan (لن نسافرَ أبداً) .
lan (لن)+ subjunctive mood

Imperative — lā (لا) *not* + jussive mood (see pp. 133-4 in *What is the Imperative Mood?*)

Affirmative ***Tell** him everything.*
qul la-hu kull-a s͟hay'i-n (قل له كل شيء).
imperative mood

Negative ***Don't tell** him anything.*
lā taqul la-hu shay'-a-n (لا تقلْ له شيئاً).
jussive mood

Perfect — lam (لم) *has not, did not* + jussive mood

Affirmative *Have you seen him?*
hal **ra'ay-ta**-hu (هل رأيته؟)?
perfect

Negative *I haven't seen him yet.*
lam 'ara-hu baʿdu (لم أراه بعد).
lam (لم) + jussive mood

Negative "to be" — Although Arabic does not express the verb *to be* in the present affirmative, it does express *to be* in the present negative. The verb **laysa** (ليس) *not to be* conjugated in the perfect tense has present time meaning.

Affirmative *Tunisia [is] in Africa.*
tūnis-u fī 'afrīqiyā (تونس في افريقيا) .
subject predicate

Negative *Tunisia **is not** in Asia.*
lays-at tūnis-u fī 'āsiyā (ليست تونس في آسيا).
perfect 3rd pers. fem. sing.

Consult your textbook for other uses of **lays-a** (ليس) and the other negatives.

DECLARATIVE AND INTERROGATIVE

IN ENGLISH

A declarative sentence can be changed to an interrogative sentence in one of two ways:

- by placing the appropriate form of the auxiliary verb *to do* before the subject + the dictionary form of the main verb.

  Declarative It *looks* difficult.
  present

  Interrogative *Does* it *look* difficult?
  present *to do* + dictionary form of *to look*

  Declarative They *liked* the car.
  past

  Interrogative *Did* they *like* the car?
  past *to do* + dictionary form of *to like*

- by inverting the normal word order of subject + verb to verb + subject. This **INVERSION** process is used with auxiliary verbs or modals (see *What are Auxiliary Verbs?*, p. 99).

Declarative *Zaynab is* still a student.
Interrogative *Is Zaynab* still a student?

Declarative *They were playing* tennis.
Interrogative *Were they playing* tennis?

Declarative *They will come* tomorrow.
Interrogative *Will they come* tomorrow?

IN ARABIC

A declarative sentence can be changed to an interrogative sentence in several ways, depending on whether it is an affirmative or negative sentence.

Affirmative sentences — An affirmative declarative sentence can be made interrogative several ways:

- by adding **hal** (هل) *(is it the case that...?)* at the beginning of the sentence (see p. 000):

  Declarative *Layla [is] truly beautiful.*
  laylā jamīlat-u-n ḥaqqan (ليلى جميلةٌ حقاً).
  Interrogative *[Is] Layla truly beautiful?*
  hal laylā jamīlat-u-n ḥaqq-a-n? (هل ليلى جميلةٌ حقاً؟)

- by adding an interrogative word such as **man** (من) *who?* **matā** (متى) *when?*, **li-mādhā** (لماذا) *why?*, **kayfa** (كيف) *how?*, etc. at the beginning of the sentence:

  Declarative *She came from Basra.*
  ḥaḍar-at min -l-baṣrat-i (حضرت من البصرة).
  Interrogative ***When** did she come from Basra?*
  matā ḥaḍar-at min -l-baṣrat-i? (متى حضرت من البصرة؟)

Negative sentences — A negative declarative sentence can be made interrogative by adding **'a** *(is it the case that...?)* to the first word.

Declarative *The director hasn't come yet.*
lam ya'ti -l-mudīr-u baᶜdu. (لم يأت المدير بعدُ)
Interrogative *Hasn't the director come yet?*
'**a**-lam ya'ti -l-mudīr-u baᶜdu ? (ألم يأت المدير بعد؟)

TAGS

In both English and Arabic, when you expect a yes-or-no answer, you can also transform an affirmative or negative statement into a question by adding a short phrase called a TAG.

IN ENGLISH

There are many different tags, depending on the tense of the verb of the statement and whether the statement is affirmative or negative. For instance, negative statements take affirmative tags and affirmative statements take negative tags.

Interrogative negative statement	The Arab armies *didn't reach* India, *did they?* (*didn't reach*: negative; *did they?*: affirmative)
Interrogative affirmative statement	But they *did reach* Iran, *didn't they?* (*did reach*: affirmative; *didn't they?*: negative)

IN ARABIC

There is only one tag which can be added at the end of an affirmative or negative statement expecting a yes-or-no answer → **'a-lays-a ka<u>dh</u>ālika** (أليس كذلك؟)? *(is it not so?).*

Declarative	*Our teacher is Palestinian.* muᶜallimu-nā filasṭīniyy-u-n. (معلمنا فلسطيني)
Interrogative	*Our teacher is Palestinian,* ***isn't he?*** muᶜallimu-nā filasṭīniyy-u-n, **'a-laysa ka<u>dh</u>ālika**? (معلمنا فلسطيني، أليس كذلك؟)

CHAPTER

47

WHAT IS MEANT BY DIRECT AND INDIRECT STATEMENTS?

A **DIRECT STATEMENT** is the transmission of a message between a speaker and a listener. The message is set in quotation marks.

> Fuad says, "I am a student."
> Akram said, "I am a student."

An **INDIRECT STATEMENT** is the reporting of a message without quoting the exact words of the message.

> Fuad says that he is a student.
> Akram said that he was a student.

IN ENGLISH

When a direct statement is changed to an indirect statement the words between quotation marks have to be adapted to reported speech.

1. The words between the quotation marks become a subordinate clause introduced by *that*. Since *that* is frequently omitted in English, we have put it between parentheses.
2. Pronouns, possessive adjectives and verbs are changed to reflect the change of speaker.
3. Verb tenses are shifted in order to maintain the logical time sequence.

Direct Akram *said*, "I *work* as a reporter."
said: past; *work*: present
↓
Indirect Akram *said* [that] he *worked* as a reporter.
said: past; *worked*: past

Direct Akram *said*, "I *worked* as a reporter."
said: past; *worked*: past
↓
Indirect Akram *said* [that] he *had worked* as a reporter.
said: past; *had worked*: past perfect

Direct Akram *said*, "I *will work* as a reporter."
said: past; *will work*: past
↓
Indirect Akram *said* [that] he *would work* as a reporter.
said: past; *would work*: future-in-the-past

IN ARABIC

As in English, direct statements are usually placed between quotation marks. When a direct statement is changed to an indirect statement, the words between quotation marks are adapted to reported speech in the following way:

1. As in English, the reported statement is introduced by *that.* While *that* can be omitted in English [between brackets in the examples below], the Arabic equivalent must be expressed in one of two ways: after the verb **qāl-a** (قال) *he said (to say)* → **’inna** (إن) or after any other verb → **’anna** (أن) .
2. As in English, the pronouns in the reported statement are changed to reflect the change of speaker.
3. Unlike English, the tense of the verb of the reported statement remains the same.

Direct *Akram **said**, "I **work** as a reporter."*
past — present
qāl-a ’akram-u, "**’aʿmal-u** murāsil-a-n." (قال أكرم «اعمل مراسلاً»)
perfect — imperfect

↓

Indirect *Akram **said** [that] **he worked** as a reporter.*
past — past
qāl-a ’akram-u ’inna-hu **yaʿmal-u** murāsil-a-n.
(قال اكرم انه يعمل مراسلا)
perfect — imperfect

Direct *Akram **said**, "I **worked** as a reporter."*
past — past
qāl-a ’akram-u, "**ʿamil-tu** murāsil-a-n." (قال أكرم «عملتُ مراسلاً»)
perfect — perfect

↓

Indirect *Akram **said** [that] **he had worked** as a reporter.*
past — past perfect
qāl-a ’akram-u inna-hu **ʿamil-a** murāsil-a-n. (قال اكرم انه عمل مراسلا)
perfect — perfect

Direct *Akram **said**, "I **will work** as a reporter."*
past — future
qāl-a ’akram-u, "**sawfa ’aʿmal-u** murāsil-a-n." (قال أكرم «سوف اعمل مراسلاً»)
perfect — future

↓

Indirect *Akram **said** [that] **he would work** as a reporter.*
past — future-in-the-past
qāl-a ’akram-u inna-hu **sawfa yaʿmal-u** murāsil-a-n.
(قال اكرم انه سوف يعمل مراسلا)
perfect — future

CHAPTER

48

WHAT IS MEANT BY DIRECT AND INDIRECT QUESTIONS?

A **DIRECT QUESTION** is the transmission of a question between a speaker and a listener. The question is set in quotation marks.

> Suhayl asked, "When does the party start?"
> Samar wondered, " Where is the party?"

An **INDIRECT QUESTION** is the reporting of a question without quoting the exact words of the message.

> Suhayl asked when the party would start.
> Samar wondered where the party was.

IN ENGLISH

When a direct question is changed to an indirect question the words between quotation marks have to be adapted to reported speech.

1. The words between the quotation marks become a subordinate clause introduced by the same interrogative word that introduced the question.
2. Pronouns, possessive adjectives and the verb are changed to reflect the change of speaker.
3. Verb tenses are shifted in order to maintain the logical time sequence.
4. A question expecting a yes-or-no answer is introduced by *if* or *whether.*

Direct Ali *asked,* "Who *is coming* to the party?"
(*asked*: past; *is coming*: present)
↓
Indirect Ali *asked* who *was coming* to the party.
(*asked*: past; *was coming*: past)

Direct Ali *asked,* "Where *was* the party?"
(*asked*: past; *was*: past)
↓
Indirect Ali *asked* where the party *had been.*
(*asked*: past; *had been*: past perfect)

Direct Ali *wondered,* "How *did I miss* the party?"
(*wondered*: past; *did I miss*: past)
↓
Indirect Ali *wondered* how *he had missed* the party.
(*wondered*: present; *he had missed*: past perfect)

Direct yes-or-no answer — Ali *wonders*, "*Was I invited?*"
(wonders: present; Was I invited: past)

Indirect yes-or-no answer — Ali *wonders whether he had been invited.*
(wonders: present; had been invited: past perfect)

IN ARABIC

As in English, direct questions are usually placed between quotation marks. When a direct question is changed to an indirect question, the words between quotation marks are adapted to reported speech in the following way:

1. As in English, the reported question is introduced by the same interrogative word that introduced the direct question.
2. As in English, the pronouns in the reported question are changed to reflect the change of speaker.
3. Unlike English, the tense of the verb of the reported question remains the same.
4. In Arabic, when a direct question expecting a yes-or-no answer is changed to an indirect question, the initial word of the direct question, **hal** (هل), is replaced by **'idhā** (إذا) *if* or **ᶜam-mā 'idhā** (عما إذا) *if, whether*.

Direct *Ali* ***asked***, *"Where [****is****] the party?"*
(asked: past; is: present)

sa'al-a ᶜaliyy-u-n "'ayna -l-ḥaflat-u?" (سأل علي «أين الحفلة»)
(sa'al-a: perfect; 'ayna -l-ḥaflat-u: present)

Indirect *Ali* ***asked*** *where the party* ***was.***
(asked: past; was: present)

sa'al-a ᶜaliyy-u-n 'ayna -l-ḥaflat-u. (سأل علي اين الحفلة)
(sa'al-a: perfect; 'ayna -l-ḥaflat-u: present)

Direct *Ali* ***asked***, *"Where* ***was*** *the party?"*
(asked: past; was: past)

sa'al-a ᶜaliyy-u-n, "'ayna **kān-at** -l-ḥaflat-u?" (سأل علي «أين كانت الحفلة؟»)
(sa'al-a: perfect; kān-at: perfect)

Indirect *Ali* ***asked*** *where the party* ***had been.***
(asked: past; had been: past → past perfect)

sa'al-a ᶜaliyy-u-n 'ayna **kān-at** -l-ḥaflat-u. (سأل علي اين كانت الحفلة)
(sa'al-a: perfect; kān-at: perfect)

Direct

*Ali **asked**, "Where **will** the party **be?**"*

past — future

sa'al-a ʿaliyy-u-n, "'ayna **sa-takūn-u** -l-ḥaflat-u?" (سأل علي «أين ستكون الحفلة؟»)

perfect — future

↓

Indirect

*Ali **asked** where the party **would be.***

past — future → future in the past

sa'al-a ʿaliyy-u-n 'ayna **sa-takūn-u** -l-ḥaflat-u. (سأل علي اين ستكون الحفلة)

perfect — future

Direct
yes-no-answer

*Ali **wonders**, "**Was I invited?**"*

present — past

yatasā'al-u ʿaliyy-u-n, "hal **kun-tu** madʿu-ww-a-n?" (يتساءل علي " هل كنت مدعوا؟")

imperfect — perfect

↓

Indirect

*Ali **wonders** whether **he had been invited.***

present — past → past perfect

yatasā'al-u ʿaliyy-u-n ʿammā 'i<u>dh</u>ā **kāna** madʿu-ww-a-n. (يتساءل علي عما إذا كان مدعوا)

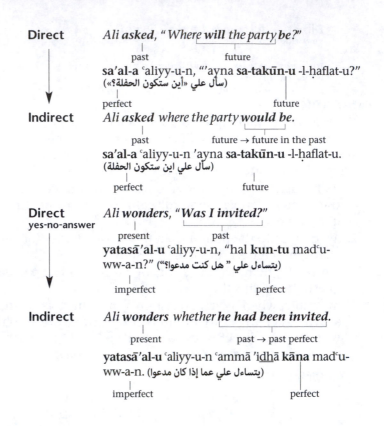

imperfect — perfect

a, an 26
abstract noun 11, 27
accusative case 23, 62
active participle 96
active voice 123
adjectives 40-1
adverbs 138-9
affirmative sentence 163, 156
agent in passive sentence 123
agreement 9
'an (أن)+ subjunctive 142, 143
'anna (أنّ) + indicative 142, 143, 159
antecendent 55, 77
Arabic alphabet 3
articles 25-8
attributive adjective 42
auxiliary verbs 99-102
'ayy-u-n (أيّ) which? 52

broken plural 18, 24

case 20-4
clauses 146-7
collective noun 18
commands (direct/indirect) 131
common noun 11
comparative degree 45
comparison of adjectives 45-9
compound/complex sentence 147
compound tense 99, 105
concrete noun 11, 27, 28
condition clause 149
conditional sentences 149-52
conjugation 90-4, 107
conjunctions 140-4
contextual form 3
contrary-to-fact 128, 150
coordinating conjunction 140

dangling preposition 66
declarative sentence 153
declension 24, 46-9
definite article 25
demonstrative adjectives 40, 54
demonstrative phrase 73
demonstrative pronouns 56, 72-6
demonstrative pronoun table 74
derived verb 85
descriptive adjectives 40, 42-4
dictionary form of noun 12
dictionary form of verb 86
direct object 36
dual noun 17

elative pattern 46
emphasis 61, 71, 107, 110
English/Arabic corresponding tenses 103
equational sentence: see verbless sentence

feminine gender 14
feminine suffix **-at-** 8, 14
flash cards 2
Form system of Arabic verbs 85
functions of words 9, 20
future in the past 115
future of probability 114
future perfect tense 119
future prefix **sa- (sawfa)** (س) (سوف) 113
future tense verbs 113-6

gender 13-5
genitive case 23
genitive case (in pronouns) 68
genitive case pronoun table 51
genitive construct **(da¯fa)** (إضافة) 23, 30, 52
gerunds see infinitives/gerunds
glottal stop **(hamza)** (همزة) 7, 25, 84

he 57
him, her 62
himself, herself 70
his, her 50
his, hers 68 I 57

idiom 5
if 152
imperative mood formation 132
imperative mood 126, 131-4
imperfect tense conjugation 91, 107
indefinite article 26
indefinite noun 26
independent pronoun 56, 58

indicative mood 126
indirect object 36
indirect question 160
indirect statements 158-9 infinitives and gerunds 93-4 infix 7
inflection 22, 91
interjection 6
interrogative adjectives 40, 52-3
interrogative pronouns 55, 65-7
interrogative sentence 155
irregular verb 88
it 57
"it" 59
its 50, 68
itself 70

jussive mood 127, 134, 154, 155
jussive conjugation 133

ka¯n-a (كان) as auxiliary 100

lays-a (ليس) not to be 155
li- (لِ) belonging to 68
linking verb 34, 42

main clause 77
main verb 99
masculine gender 13
me 62
mine 68
my 50
myself 70
modal verb 101
mood 126-7

negative command 133
negative sentence 153
neuter gender 14
nominative case 22
nominative case pronoun table 58
non-human plural noun 60
noun of unity 19
noun 11-12
noun-preposition 136
number 16-19
nunation 26

object of preposition 39
object pronouns 62-4
objective case 22, 62
objects 21, 36-9
of 29
our 50
ours 69
ourselves 70

part of speech 5
participles (verbal adjectives) 95-8
participial phrase 145
particle 6
passive participle 97
passive pattern 124
passive voice 123
past habitual meaning 111
past imperfect conjugation 110
past participle 95
past perfect tense 118
past progressive 122
past tense verbs 109-12
pattern 8
pausal form 3
perfect tense conjugation 109
perfect tenses 117-20
perfective particle **qad** (قد) 104, 117,120
personal pronoun 55
person (in verbs) 57
phrases 145-6
plural noun 16
positive degree 45
possession 29
possessive adjectives 40, 50-1
possessive case 22
possessive pronouns 56, 68-9
possessives 29-31
possible condition 149
predicate adjective 42. 44
predicates 21, 34-5
prefix 6, 91
prepositional phrase 135 prepositions 135-7
present participle 95
present perfect tense 117
present tense verbs 106-8
principal parts of verbs 88-9
progressive meaning in Arabic 121
progressive tenses 121-2
pronoun, subjective case 57-8
pronouns 55-6

proper noun 11
questions (direct/indirect) 160-2
radical 7
reflexive pronouns 55, 70-1
relative clause 77
relative pronouns 56, 77-83
relative pronoun table 81
result clause 149
root 7
sentences (affirmative, negative, declarative, interrogative) 153-7
sentences 147-8
shall: see *will*
she 57
simple tense 105
singular noun 16
sound plural 17, 24
stem of word 6, 12, 91, 106
stem vowel 89, 106
Study Guide 1
subject in verbal sentence 33, 35
subject in verbless sentence 34
subject pronouns 57-61
subject 21
subjective case 21
subjects 32-3
subjective case 57
subjunctive conjugation 129
subjunctive mood 126, 128-30
subordinate clause 77, 140
subordinating conjunction 140
suffix 6, 91
suffixed pronoun 56
suffixed pronoun, genitive case 51
superlative degree 46, 49

tags 156
tenses 103-5
the 25
their 50
theirs 69
them 62
themselves 70
they 57
"they" 60
this, that 54, 72
three-case declension 24, 47
to be 99
to do 100
to have 99
transitivity 87

two-case declension 46

used to 112
verb conjugation 90-2
verb phrase 86, 145
verb-subject agreement 33
verbal nouns **(mas.dar)** (مصدر) 89, 94
verbal sentence 33, 35, 61, 146
verbless (equational) sentence 34, 43, 60, 61, 147
verbs 84-7
voice (active/passive) 123-5

we 57
what? 65
which? 52
who?, whom? 65
whose? 53, 65
will 101, 105, 113, 119
word function 20
word order 21
word pattern 8
would 101, 112, 115

you 57, 62
"you" 58
your 50
yours 68, 69
yourself, yourselves 70